Memories and History of Parole Area – Annapolis and Anne Arundel County, Maryland

By Members, Friends, and Supporters
of the Parole Rotary Club
Annapolis, Maryland

Copyright © 2019 by Parole Rotary
and individual contributors.

All rights reserved.

ISBN 978-1-62806-224-3

Libray of Congress Control Number 2019940981

Published by Salt Water Media
29 Broad Street, Suite 104
Berlin, MD 21811
www.saltwatermedia.com

Cover design by Salt Water Media

Interior photographs used courtesy
of Parole Rotary and Les Howard Studios

Rotary Four-Way Test

1. Is it the truth?

2. Is it fair to all concerned?

3. Will it build good will and better friendships?

4. Will it be beneficial to all concerned?

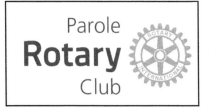 We are sharing memories of persons who live here, and those who have lived here, along with oral history passed down from ancestors.

We hope you find the stories about the area covering about 400 years intriguing and enjoyable. Profits from the sale of this book will go toward the community service projects of the Parole Rotary Club.

Rotary is the oldest service organization in the world.

Parole is a neighborhood of Annapolis, Maryland, rich in history and tradition. Parole was an economic and neighborhood development area, with a race track for thoroughbred horses. The name comes from Camp Parole, the Civil War prisoner-of-war parolee exchange camp, but the history of the area goes back hundreds of years before that. Parole was originally a part of Anne Arundel County prior to being annexed by the City of Annapolis in 1951.

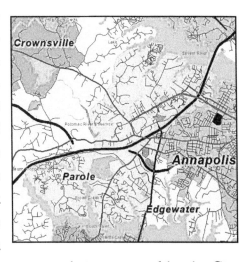

Memories and History of Parole Area Annapolis and Anne Arundel County, Maryland

Table of Contents

How To Purchase This Book i
Acknowledgements ii
Introduction iv
Letter from Rhonda Pindell Charles, Ward 3 Alderwoman, City of Annapolis v

Part I: Parole Area

Parole: Historical Roots 1
    Plaques under the New Three Mile Oak Tree 2
    Maryland's State Tree: The White Oak 2
    Four Signers of the Declaration of Independence from Maryland 3
    Charles Carroll 3
    Samuel Chase 3
    William Paca 4
    Thomas Stone 5
Annapolis 7
    Meeting of the Confederation Congress 7
    George Washington's Commission Resignation 7
    Treaty of Paris Signing and Ratification 8
    The Annapolis Convention 8
Parole's History with the Thoroughbred Horse 10

- Maryland's State Horse: The Thoroughbred 12
- Tale of a Thoroughbred Horse Named Parole 13
- George Washington in Parole and Annapolis 16
- The United States Naval Academy 20
  - The Navy Hymn: "Eternal Father, Strong to Save" 24
- Union Soldiers in Parole 27
  - For More Information about Camp Parole 33
- President Abraham Lincoln in Annapolis via Parole 34
  - For More Information about President Lincoln's Trip to Annapolis 36
- Marylanders Benjamin Banneker and Frederick Douglass 37
  - Mount Moriah AME Church 37
  - Benjamin Banneker 38
  - Frederick Douglass 40
- Public Servants Representing Parole 43
  - William Butler, Sr., and William Butler, Jr. 43
  - Thomas Norwood Brown 44
  - John T. Chambers, Jr. 44
  - Samuel Gilmer 45
  - Classie Gillis Hoyle 46
  - Rhonda Pindell Charles 47
- Railroads into Annapolis and Camp Parole 49
- Parole Churches 51
- Parole Schools 56
  - Legal, Historical, and Constitutional Issues Involving Education and Civil Rights 59
  - For More Information on Parole Schools 63

Parole Cemeteries 64
Memories of Parole 68
    Katherine Joyce 68
    Pearl Swann 69
    Alma Wright Cropper 70
    Bess Demas: Open Gate Restaurant and Hotel 71
    Dave Finkelstein and Ron and Marilyn Snyder: From Finkelsteins to Snyder's Antiques to Return to Oz 73
    Lorna Cunningham: Shady Oaks Inn 76
    Sports Teams in Parole 79
Drs. Faye Allen and Aris T. Allen and the Parole Health Center 80
Aris T. Allen Memorial 83
Thomas Somerville Company 85
Bowen's Farm Supply 89
Light House Shelter and Light House Bistro 91
Gardner Center 93
Paul Bunyan Statue 94
Parole Plaza Shopping Center 95
Gresham House 98
London Town 101
Public Gardens in the Area Open to the Public 103
Annapolis and Anne Arundel County Public Boat Ramps ... 104
Carr's and Sparrow's Beaches (1926-1974) 105
    Charles Walker "Hoppy" Adams and WANN Radio Station 106

Kunta Kinta/Alex Haley (KKAH) Monument and Foundation 109

Pieces of Parole 111

    For More Information about Life in Parole 113

The Greater Parole Community Association and Tree Planting 114

How the Streets in Parole Got Their Names 116

    For More Information about the History of Parole 123

Part II: Historical Background

Dodon Plantation (now Dodon Farm) 124

Patuxent River 126

Maryland Nicknames 128

    The Old Line State 128

    The Free State 129

Maryland State Flag 131

Maryland State Song: "Maryland, My Maryland" 133

The National Anthem: "The Star-Spangled Banner" 136

Namesakes 139

    State of Maryland 139

    Sixteen Counties in Maryland with English Roots and Namesakes 140

    Anne Arundel County 142

    City of Annapolis 144

Royal House of Stewart or Stuart 146

    Beginnings in Scotland 146

    Continuation in England 147

Maryland Census of 1860 and 2010 153
    Maryland Census of 1860 153
    Maryland Census of 2010 153
The Terrible Cost of the Civil War 154
President Abraham Lincoln: His Family and His Legacy 156
    President Lincoln and His Family in Illinois, Kentucky, and Washington, D.C. 156
    President Lincoln's Legislative Legacy 160
    The Lincoln Family Post Civil War 161

Part III: Parole Rotary Club

Rotary Club of Parole (Annapolis) Maryland, Inc. 166
    History of the Rotary Club 166
    Rotary Motto: Service above Self 166
    Projects of the Parole Rotary Club 167
    Parole Rotary Club's Mission 172
    Parole Rotary Club's Vision 172
Books for International Goodwill (B.I.G.): A BIG Project 173
Naptown barBAYq Contest and Music Festival 175
Closing 178

Appendix: Favorite Recipes from the Rotary Club

Traditional Maryland Recipes 179
    Southern Maryland Stuffed Ham 179
    Southern Maryland Fried Oysters 180
    Maryland Oyster Stew 180
    Rockfish 181

Crab Cakes	181
Londontown Terrace Crab Pie	182
Carrot Fritters	183
Old Time Roast Wild Duck	184
Recipes Using Fresh Produce	185
Squash Casserole	185
Tomato Casserole	186
Meatball and Vegetable Casserole	187
Gazpacho	188
Bread-Tomato Casserole (Brot-Tomaten Auflaue)	189
Cranberry-Apple Crisp	190
Other Favorite Recipes	191
Black Max Barbecue Sauce	191
Grilled Pork Sausage with Warm Potato Salad	192
Southern Spoon Bread	193
Baked Grits	194
Mexican Spaghetti	195
Taco Cheese Ball	196
Sauerkraut and Pork (Alsatian)	197
Pumpkin-Pecan Spice Bread	198

About the Researcher/Editor/Author – Joyce Edelson 199

How To Purchase This Book:

To purchase additional copies of *Memories and History of Parole Area – Annapolis and Anne Arundel County, Maryland*, contact the Parole Rotary Club via e-mail at parolerotary@gmail.com or visit our website at www.Parole-Rotary.org.

Acknowledgements

Thank you to all who participated in this community effort recognizing the wealth of history in the area of Anne Arundel County and the city of Annapolis known as Parole and surrounding areas. We are grateful to all who shared historical stories, memories, tidbits and family recipes to make this a truly unique book.

Carla Downs, whose family has lived in Parole for several generations, offered invaluable assistance in introducing this book's researcher/editor, Joyce Edelson, to many people, places, and events in the history of Parole. Carla serves on the Board of Directors of the Greater Parole Community Association, and was generous in sharing her own memories of Parole.

The Maryland State Archives, 350 Rowe Boulevard, Annapolis, was a great resource for history and photographs. A variety of sources was used in writing this book and cited when possible.

A special thank you goes out to Rotarians Dave Vogel for managing the project and Les Goldberg of Les Howard Studios for providing photo editing and original images. Les is an award winning photographer who makes his home between Annapolis, Maryland and Palm Coast, Florida. For more information on Les Goldberg and Les Howard Studios visit https://www.leshowardstudios.com/.

And a thank you goes to proofreaders Frank Peterson, Jane Frantzich, Sue Taylor, Jim Ohler, Robert Smith and Mike Roblyer.

We appreciate the professional copy editing services donated by Dr. Pamela W. Roblyer.

We are grateful for the leadership of the Presidents of the Parole Rotary Club who shepherded this book to its completion: Scott Meyers, Robert Smith, Henry Riser and Dave Vogel.

We tried to be as accurate as we could in interpreting the

available research, all the while being respectful of our neighbors in Parole who shared their lives. When possible, we cited all historical stories. The legacy of those who have been a part of Parole's history will long be remembered and honored through oral and written histories. Any errors were inadvertent and we ask your understanding of the effort and dedication to the process of sharing citizens' experiences for this book, and to please forgive any trespasses.

Joyce Edelson, editor, continues to collect stories from anyone interested in sharing their memories and experiences involving Parole. She can be reached via e-mail at JoyceEdelson@gmail.com.

Thank you for purchasing this book and helping the Parole Rotary Club make a difference in our community.

Introduction

The original Parole area was bound by Chinquapin Round Road and Old Solomon's Road and Route 2, Admiral Cochrane Drive, and Poplar Drive in Annapolis, although the boundaries have now extended east through several neighborhoods beyond Chinquapin Round Road, south to Harry Truman Drive, west to Riva Road, and north to Bestgate Road.

The Rotary Club of Parole (Annapolis) Maryland, Inc., commonly referred to as the Parole Rotary Club, is building on several previous works to tell more of the history and stories of the community known as Parole.

The Parole Rotary Club, a community service organization, meets every Tuesday morning at 7:30 a.m. in the Doubletree Hotel, 210 Holiday Court, off Riva Road in Parole, a few blocks from where Camp Parole stood. Attend a meeting as our guest. Join us for breakfast, fellowship, and hearing a speaker on all manner of subjects. One hundred percent of the profits from this book will go to Parole Rotary's community service efforts.

Parole Welcome Sign
Image courtesy of Les Howard Studios

Letter from Rhonda Pindell Charles, Ward 3 Alderwoman, City of Annapolis

To members of the Parole Rotary Club, Annapolis, Maryland:

Thank you for researching, writing and publishing this book, *Memories and History of Parole Area – Annapolis and Anne Arundel County, Maryland*.

You have captured the nearly 400-year history and spirit of our community nicely.

The beginning stories relate our colonial history of horse racing, with George Washington sometimes in attendance, the Continental Congress held here and attended by many of our founding fathers, the Naval Academy, and the story of Camp Parole, the Civil War prisoner-of-war exchange camp from which our community derives its name.

The stories of Abraham Lincoln's trip through here toward the end of the Civil War and public servants from the beginning to the present who have represented our community on various city councils and the Maryland state legislature provide interesting pieces of our history. The difficult journey of overcoming the legacy of slavery, segregation, and the battle for adequate health care are captured in a respectful manner. Of particular importance is the educational role our schools, students, teachers, and principals played on the local and national stage. The references of schools, churches, cemeteries, and the street index will be helpful to everyone in the area.

It was delightful reading the memories of growing up in Parole, many of which mirrored my own, as well as those who established businesses in the area.

Seeing Parole in the context of how the neighborhood fits into our city, county, state, and national governments is enlightening. We are all very proud of our city, county, and state, which makes the stories of how Parole became what it is today more than just a trip down memory lane.

I am pleased that the community was able to facilitate and assist in the process.

Sincerely,
Rhonda Pindell Charles
Ward 3 Alderwoman, City of Annapolis, State of Maryland

Part I: Parole Area

White Oak Tree

Parole: Historical Roots

A white oak tree stood three miles from Maryland's state capital in the area that would become known as Parole. Under this tree, called the Three Mile Oak, General George Washington passed en route to Annapolis on December 19, 1783, to resign his commission as Commander-in-Chief of the Continental Armies to the Continental Congress, then seated in Annapolis. A commemorative plaque, erected in 1967 by the Four Rivers Garden Club, has been relocated to a triangular plot of land beside Route 450 (West Street) and Jennifer Road near the Routes 50 and 301 overpass, about two-tenths of a mile from the original white oak tree and greeting point three miles from the state capital located in Annapolis. The original tree was taken down after being hit by lightning. A new white oak tree was planted close to the relocated plaques to perpetuate the memory of the original Three Mile Oak in Parole.

Plaques under the New Three Mile Oak Tree
Two plaques under the tree provide the following information:
Upper Plaque: This oak tree planted in 1967 perpetuates the memory of the original Three Mile Oak which stood nearby as explained in the marker below.
Lower Plaque: Under this tree passed General George Washington December 19, 1783, on his way to Annapolis to resign his commission as Commander-in-Chief of the Continental Armies; and it is thought that General Smallwood accompanied by General Gates and distinguished citizens of Annapolis met General Washington at this spot. General Lafayette passed here December 17, 1824, to visit with friends of the revolutionary days.

Maryland's State Tree: The White Oak
The white oak was named Maryland's state tree in 1941. Some are known to have lived for more than 600 years. Native to eastern North America, they can reach heights of 60 to 150 feet, with trunk diameters between 3 and 4 feet. Trees around 50 years old begin producing acorns, as many as 10,000 annually. These acorns are sweet and have been a dietary mainstay for over 80 species of birds and mammals. Native Americans ground acorns into flour, as did early European settlers. It is unusual to see these trees with white bark, their usual color being ashen to dark gray. White oaks produce durable and beautiful hardwood lumber with a fine, almost watertight grain.

Source: www.maryland.gov

Four Signers of the Declaration of Independence from Maryland

Four signers of the Declaration of Independence came from Maryland. All four were lawyers, all four were slave owners, and all four of their homes in Annapolis have been preserved. Of the 56 men who signed the Declaration of Independence, only 15 of their homes are still standing, four of which are located in Annapolis.

Charles Carroll

Charles Carroll, known as Charles Carroll of Carrollton was born in 1737 into a wealthy Roman Catholic family of Annapolis and was formally educated at a Jesuit College in France, where he lived from the ages of 8 to 20. After returning to America in 1773 amidst the growing revolt against English taxation of the colonies, he immediately became active as a representative to many of the early

Charles Carroll

conventions and served in elective office until retirement. He was the last surviving signer of the Declaration and is believed to be the only Catholic to sign. His home has been preserved along Spa Creek, next to St. Mary's Church in Annapolis. Carroll died at the age of 95 in 1832.

Samuel Chase

Chase, born in 1741 in Princess Anne (Somerset County) on the Eastern Shore of Maryland, received his education in law in Baltimore and represented Maryland at the Continental Congress.

Samuel Chase

In 1786 he moved to Baltimore, presided in criminal courts there, and was later appointed chief justice of the state. In 1796, George Washington appointed him to the Supreme Court of the United States. He began construction of a home on Maryland Avenue in Annapolis, but was unable to finish the construction and sold the unfinished house to Edward Lloyd IV of Wye Plantation on the Eastern Shore. It is now known as the Chase-Lloyd House. Chase died in 1800.

Historical Sidebar: In 1802, **Francis Scott Key** *married Mary "Polly" Tayloe Lloyd in the dining room of the Chase-Lloyd House. They had 12 children.*

William Paca

Paca was born in 1740 in Abington (Harford County), was educated at Philadelphia College, and studied law in Annapolis and in England. He was elected to the Maryland state legislature and appointed to the Continental Congress, served as chief justice of the State of Maryland, was elected governor of Maryland, and was then appointed a federal district judge for the State of Maryland. His home on Prince George Street has been preserved. Paca died in 1799.

William Paca

Thomas Stone

Stone, born in 1743 in Charles County, was educated by a Scottish school master and studied law at the office of Thomas Johnson, a delegate to the Continental Congress and an Associate Justice of the Supreme Court of the United States. Stone began practicing law in Frederick, Maryland, and was elected to Congress before and again after the Revolutionary War. He was a member of the committee that framed the Articles of Confederation. Thomas Stone and his family lived in the home he owned in Annapolis from 1783 to 1787, known as the Peggy Stewart House, located near the Naval Academy and now privately owned.

Thomas Stone

The ship *Peggy Stewart*, named after the daughter of Captain Anthony Stewart who once owned both house and ship, is famous for its part in the "Annapolis Tea Party" during the American Revolutionary War. Its cargo consisted of goods, tea, and 53 indentured servants. After three months, Stewart negotiated an agreement to pay the tax so he could unload its cargo. The ship was burned in the Annapolis harbor in 1774 by town "patriots," who were in favor of not paying any taxes to England. The burning took place almost a year after the more famous Boston Tea Party. The ruins of the ship now lie beneath reclaimed land under Luce Hall at the Naval Academy. Francis Blackwell Mayer painted "The Burning of the Peggy Stewart," and an artist's rendering of the ship is in the Maritime Committee research files.

The plantation home Stone built in Port Tobacco, Charles County, Maryland, about 50 miles south of Annapolis was restored after a devastating fire in 1977, assuring its preservation. Stone died in 1787.

Historical Sidebar: Mary Katherine Goddard (1783-1816) of Baltimore, Maryland, was the second printer of the Constitution, sometimes known as the "Goddard Broadside." She was the first female  *postmaster in the colonies in 1775, and ran the Baltimore Post Office, a bookstore, a print shop, and a newspaper. Her copy of the Constitution was commissioned by Congress in 1777 and was the first to include the names of the signatories. At the bottom appear these words in small print: "Baltimore, in Maryland: Printed by Mary Katherine Goddard."*

Mary Katherine Goddard

Source: www.maryland.gov

Annapolis

Meeting of the Confederation Congress
The city of Annapolis played a significant role during the founding of the government, and the nation's Founding Fathers walked the city streets. With the Revolutionary War over, the hard work of creating a government for the new nation had begun. Initially the new country was governed under the Articles of Confederation, which the founding fathers realized was inadequate to solve the problems of the young country, specifically the need for a strong central government and the need to raise funds to run the government.

Meetings of the Confederation Congress were held at numerous locations, with Annapolis being one of them. The Confederation Congress met at the Maryland State House in Annapolis from November 26, 1783, to August 19, 1784. It was while they were in Annapolis that George Washington resigned his commission as Commander-in-Chief of the Continental Armies on Tuesday, December 23, 1783. Washington was met outside of town beside a white oak tree located three miles from the State House. He was accompanied into town by two trusted aides, David Humphreys and Trench Tilghman. He strode into the Assembly Chamber of the Maryland State House in Annapolis, where the Congress met. Congress met in Annapolis since fleeing its own mutinous troops in Philadelphia, the customary seat of government. History records that only 20 members representing but seven states remained in attendance at the little respected and largely ineffectual Confederation Congress.

George Washington's Commission Resignation
Following a script prepared by Thomas Jefferson, George Washington

addressed the civilian leaders and delegates of Congress and returned to them the signed commission they had voted him back in June of 1775 at the beginning of the conflict. Returning his commission ensured civilian power over the military. Washington then took his leave and returned to his home and family at Mount Vernon south of Alexandria, Virginia, on the Potomac River. He had promised his wife Martha that he would be home in time to celebrate Christmas. This significant action by George Washington showed the civilian control of the armed services.

Treaty of Paris Signing and Ratification
Based on preliminary articles with the British negotiators made on November 30, 1782, and approved by the "Congress of the Confederation" on April 15, 1783, the Treaty of Paris was further signed on September 3, 1783, and ratified by the Confederation Congress then sitting at the Maryland State House in Annapolis on January 14, 1784. This formally ended the American Revolutionary War between Great Britain and the 13 former colonies, which on July 4, 1776, had declared independence.

The Annapolis Convention
Three years later what has been called "The Annapolis Convention," then formally titled as a "Meeting of Commissioners to Remedy Defects of the Federal Government," occurred September 11 to 14, 1786, at Mann's Tavern in Annapolis (no longer existing) off Duke of Gloucester Street. Twelve delegates, including James Madison and Alexander Hamilton, from five states met to determine how to repair the deficiencies of the Articles of Confederation. Interestingly Maryland did not send a delegate. The final report of the Annapolis Convention was sent to the Congress of the Confederation and to the states. It sought support for a broader constitutional convention

to be held the following May in Philadelphia (Congress was then meeting in New York). The report expressed the hope that more states would be represented and that their delegates or deputies would be authorized to examine areas broader than simply commercial trade. Because of the few representatives in attendance, their authority was limited. As a result, other than recommending the calling of a full constitutional convention, the delegates took no action on the issues that had brought them together.

The events of the Annapolis Convention also prompted the eventual first President of the United States, George Washington, to add his plea for a stronger federal government. In a letter to fellow Founding Father James Madison dated November 5, 1786, Washington wrote, "The consequences of a lax, or inefficient government, are too obvious to be dwelt on. Thirteen Sovereignties pulling against each other and all tugging the federal hand, will soon bring ruin on the whole."[1]

The direct result of the Annapolis Convention report and the ensuing events was the Philadelphia Convention of 1787 eight months later and the drafting of the Constitution, which was later ratified by the states.

The Maryland State House is the oldest government building in continuous use and stands as a monument to events important to the early history of our country. The old Congress chamber has been renovated to show how it looked during 1783 to 1784, when it played its role as the seat of the Confederation Congress.

Source: Robert Smith, Former President of the Parole Rotary Club and Attorney

---

[1] *The Return of George Washington: Uniting the States, 1783 – 1789* by Edward J. Larson, 2014; Publisher: William Morrow Imprint of Harper Collins Publishers (as cited in The Papers of George Washington Confederation Series, Charlottesville: University Press of Virginia, 1992 – 1997, pages 83 - 84)

Parole's History with the Thoroughbred Horse

"Maryland is credited with the formal introduction of organized thoroughbred racing into the colonies," Dr. Ed Papenfuse, director of the Maryland State Archives, declared in 2003 before a Senate Committee urging the State to adopt the thoroughbred as the State Horse. The Legislature confirmed, thus paying tribute to the legacy of the noble thoroughbred history that had its beginning in Annapolis.

In 1719-1720, Mayor of Annapolis Benjamin Tasker and the town council ordered the clearing of a race track beyond the City Gate and ordered a price of 12 silver spoons, or the value of 10 pounds, the first in the Colonies, paid to the winner of the race. This action was modeled after municipal supported racing in England promoted two decades earlier by Queen Anne, Annapolis' namesake.

No one knows exactly where the Annapolis track was. Surely West Street, the entrance to the city, had been used for Match races common at the time. Historians are not sure where an oval track over natural terrain was. Some speculate that it bounded West Street near today's Loew's Hotel. But as competitive racing grew into an annual festival attended by thousands and supported by taxes on pubs, some believe it moved further out of town to an area convenient to travelers – those crossing the South River by ferry and those on the stagecoach routes from the west and north – perhaps in the farm area west of town that would later become the Parole Race Course.

Some believe this was the site where the first recorded formal horse race in Maryland was held in May of 1743. Sponsored by the Maryland Jockey Club, the oldest sporting association in North America, the race was won by an English or possibly Irish import, Dungannon, owned by George Steuart. Charles Carroll owned the horse that lost the race. Four years after the race, George Steuart purchased Dodon Plantation in Davidsonville, which is still in the Steuart family (see Part II of this book for the history of Dodon Farm).

During every war since 1776, horse racing ceased until the war's conclusion. It is likely the half-mile track was formed or revived after the Civil War. It included pacer and trotting races as well as flat race competition. But in over 100 years as a recorded track from that time it seems never to have been a profitable enterprise. The track closed and reopened many times under new owners, perhaps hooked on a memory of a distant fame in the golden years of Annapolis horse racing where thoroughbred racing began.

The site was, for a short time, the Agricultural Fair Grounds before returning to the glory of flat racing under the Parole Hunt Club. The Annapolis Towne Center at Parole is on land once owned by the Parole Hunt Club. After World War I, the Hunt Club managers

Parole Race Track

reopened the track, hoping that the "horse racing public may once again compete in the thrilling tests of stamina and speed." The Parole Hunt Club operated the track until its closing. Finally, in 1950, the on-again, off-again track was sold for a shopping center known as Parole Plaza.

Like the track before it, Parole Plaza suffered from the competition of larger and fancier competitors and eventually closed its doors. In 2008, the mixed use area of Annapolis Towne Center at Parole was opened on the once rural site that may have been home to the earliest of the colonies' thoroughbred races, where the "sport of kings" began in America.

Source: Ellen Moyer, horse enthusiast and owner, member of the Maryland Racing Commission for 4 years, and Mayor of Annapolis (2001 -2009)

Maryland's State Horse: The Thoroughbred
The average thoroughbred stands 16 hands (64 inches) high at the withers and weighs 1,000 pounds. Able to sustain speed for extended distances, thoroughbreds can run up to 40 miles per hour. They are used as racehorses and polo mounts, for show jumping and dressage, and by mounted police units and recreational riders.

Source: www.Maryland.gov

Thoroughbred Horse
Image courtesy of Les Howard Studios

Tale of a Thoroughbred Horse Named Parole

This tale has nothing to do with the neighborhood of Parole, but it is an interesting coincidence that the name of a famous thoroughbred race horse is the same as the place where the first recorded thoroughbred race in North America took place.

Parole was owned by tobacco heir Pierre Lorillard (1822-1901). Parole had an impressive breeding heritage, according to the National Museum of Racing and Hall of Fame. The brown gelding was referred to as "the Yankee mule" by writers in England who described him as light-necked, rough-coated, leggy, and curby hocked. However, what Parole lacked in looks, he more than made up for with his talent. He was born in 1873 in Pennsylvania and won races in New York, New Jersey, and Kentucky. In 1877 Parole was brought to Maryland to run in the Great Sweepstakes at Pimlico. Congress had adjourned for the day to attend, so obviously much attention accompanied the race. There were two leading contenders, and Parole was considered an afterthought. The two leading contenders exchanged leads several times amid much cheering from the crowd. As the horses turned the last quarter pole, to the apparent shock of those in attendance, Parole took the lead and won the race by five-lengths, making that race his eighth win for the year. As a five-year-old, he won the Baltimore Cup and other races for another impressive year. This led to poolrooms, saloons, and baseball clubs all being named Parole. It was suggested that this was a reminder to the Kentucky thoroughbred establishment that not all winning thoroughbreds came from Kentucky.

Lorillard took two of his horses to England in 1879. The three-year-old, often-times winner named Duke of Magenta was to be the featured runner. Parole was considered a trial horse. The featured runner became ill on the voyage across the Atlantic and never raced again, leaving Parole as Lorillard's only hope of winning in England, which he did many times. English press sports writers who wrote about Parole were no longer dismissive. American sports writers seemed to enjoy touting the prowess of one of their own against the English horses, even if the thoroughbred breed had begun in Great Britain. By the end of 1879, Parole was wearing down and stopped winning, so Lorillard brought him home to America in an attempt to resurrect his fading career. Parole rallied and won four races in 1880, and won 12 races in 1881 as an eight year old. He continued racing until age 12, but mostly Parole came in second. When Parole was finally retired at the end of 1885, his record of winnings held for many years.

Six years later, at the age of 18, Parole made a public appearance on July 4, 1891, at Monmouth Park, New Jersey. To the cheers of the crowd, Parole galloped a quarter-mile in front of the grandstand. His retirement years were spent at Lorillard's farm in New Jersey.

Parole was a friendly horse that loved company. He often stood outside a farm worker's door whinnying for attention until someone came out and spent time with him. Comfortable in his spacious paddock and keeping company with the horses Lorillard had in training, Parole died in 1903 at the age of 30. A racing historian described Parole as the most renowned gelding in the history of American racing. He was inducted into the Racing Hall of Fame in 1984.

Sources: National Museum of Racing Hall of Fame; New York Public Library

GEORGE WASHINGTON IN PAROLE AND ANNAPOLIS

Annapolis was founded in 1649, 83 years before George Washington (1732-1799) was born in Virginia. It has been estimated that Washington visited Annapolis 20 times, beginning when he was 19 years old, to see the horse races somewhere near Parole. Annapolis was already a booming place by the time Washington came to resign his commission as Commander-in-Chief of the Continental Armies, once the Revolutionary War had been won. The year was 1783, and Washington was 51 years old.

George Washington

Washington, no stranger to Annapolis and Maryland by 1783, would have remembered Maryland's 400 brave soldiers who fought at the Battle of Brooklyn during the Revolutionary War, 250 of whom died, with another 100 wounded or taken prisoner. Holding off the British regulars allowed most of Washington's troops to escape and fight another day. The history of the brave Marylanders holding that line against the British is the origin of one of Maryland's nicknames, the Old Line State (see Part II of this book).

The overland route in Maryland was about 45 miles in length. The best evidence is that Washington traveled with his horses, his coach, and his two enslaved liverymen, Giles and Paris, across the Potomac River to Maryland. The only way to cross the Potomac would have been by ferry, since the first bridge across the Potomac wasn't begun until 1833, joining Georgetown in Washington,

D.C., and Rosslyn in Arlington, Virginia. Directly opposite Mount Vernon, Washington's home on the Virginia side of the Potomac River, is Piscataway, a river and a town in Prince George's County, Maryland, which would have provided a gateway to travel throughout Maryland. His party would then have needed to find a route crossing the Patuxent River from Prince George's County to Anne Arundel County. A bridge over the Patuxent at Queen Anne Town is still aptly named Queen Anne Bridge Road, but the bridge over the Patuxent is now boarded up and no longer usable, and the town is gone from the maps. Authorized in 1706-1707, the town was big enough to be the site of a tobacco warehouse and a horse racing track. The towns around the area have been absorbed by the Patuxent River Park (see Part II of this book for history of the Patuxent River).

A second route would have been from Mount Vernon, south on the Potomac, and into Maryland at Port Tobacco, another river and town in Charles County, Maryland. Then the carriage would have followed in a northeasterly direction, probably over what is now Route 301, from Charles County to Prince George's County, and over the same Queen Anne's Bridge, crossing the Patuxent River to Anne Arundel County.

Rawlings Tavern Historical Marker
Image courtesy of Les Howard Studios

There were many plantations and taverns along the way at which to stop, such as Rawlings Tavern in Harwood (no longer existing) and plantations in Harwood, Owensville,

Galesville, and Davidsonville. Upon arrival at Londontown, in what is now Edgewater, Washington would have taken the ferry across the South River and disembarked close to Parole.

Washington bemoaned losing a pound and two shillings at the Annapolis racetrack. The United States was still a colony at that time and used the English monetary system, hence the pound and shilling reference. The system of using the dollar as the monetary unit of the United States began in 1785. The Coinage Act of 1792 introduced coinage in gold, silver, and copper. Paper notes or greenbacks were introduced into the system in 1861 to help finance the Civil War.

Washington did not raise thoroughbred race horses at his Mount Vernon plantation, but clearly had affection for horseflesh and the sound of thundering hooves.

During his presidency (1789-1797), Washington had stopped in Annapolis on his southern tour of the United States in the spring of 1791. His later visit to St. John's College elicited much excitement. His step-grandson and future father-in-law of Robert E. Lee, George Washington Parke Custis, was a member of the class of 1799. Two of his nephews also attended St. John's College.

Since the beginning of America, the Chesapeake Bay carried much traffic of people and goods north and south, so Washington may have stopped in Annapolis during those trips as well. He spent his younger years as a surveyor and again fighting in the French and Indian War in western Maryland, so Washington no doubt had affection for the state of Maryland. According to his diaries, he often had to stop and greet well-wishers during his travels around the country, which slowed his progress to wherever he was going.

An article written by Diana Dinsick in the *Bay Weekly* newspaper of December 21, 2017, references George Washington traveling via the Patuxent Ferry en route to Mount Vernon from Annapolis in December of 1783, over 234 years ago.

Sources: Historical annals; Prince George's County History pamphlet; War of 1812 annals; The Bay Weekly, December 21, 2017

The United States Naval Academy

The United States Navy began during the Revolutionary War, but declined thereafter for nearly a decade until 1794 when the first U.S. President, George Washington, persuaded Congress to authorize a new naval force to combat the growing menace of piracy on the high seas. The first vessels of the new U.S. Navy were launched in 1797. The second President, John Adams (1735-1826), built up the Navy during his presidency. In 1826, sixth President John Quincy Adams (1767-1848) urged Congress to establish a Naval Academy "for the formation of scientific and accomplished officers." However, his proposal was not acted upon until almost 20 years later.

Through the efforts of George Bancroft, Secretary of the Navy from 1880 to 1891 during the administration of 11th President James Polk, the Naval School was established without Congressional funding in October of 1845. It was reported that Secretary Bancroft, with influence from Commodore Isaac Mayo (see story in this book on the Gresham estate in Edgewater where Commodore Mayo lived), decided to move the 20-acre predecessor

U.S. Navy Flags

Bancroft Hall

naval school that had existed for seven years on Gray's Ferry Avenue in south Philadelphia to "the healthy and secluded" location of Annapolis in order to rescue midshipmen from "the temptations and distractions that necessarily connect with a large and populous city." The Philadelphia property, three buildings total, is now known as the Philadelphia Naval Asylum. The property has been designated a National Historic Landmark, primarily for its Greek Revival architecture. The buildings have been restored as luxury condominiums.

The location of the Naval Academy in Annapolis was a 10-acre Army post named Fort Severn. The first class consisted of 50 midshipmen and seven professors. During the administration of the 12th President, Zachary Taylor, the Naval School became the United States Naval Academy in 1850, and all appointments to the Naval Academy came under control of the U. S. Congress in 1852.

Once Union troops began arriving at the Naval Academy during the Civil War, the Academy was moved to Newport, Rhode Island, and continued class instruction aboard ships. By the end of the Civil War, 400 graduates had served in the Union Navy; 95

served in the Confederate Navy; and 23 graduates were killed in battle or died of wounds. The buildings at the Naval Academy in Annapolis functioned as hospitals and the first of three prisoner-of-war exchange camps. Classes resumed at the Academy once the Civil War ended.

The campus has grown to 338 acres, a third of which is landfill into the Severn River. When neighborhoods were taken over by the Naval Academy, many residents chose to move to Parole, due to the increasingly crowded downtown area in Annapolis. The Naval Academy provided many jobs for the residents of Parole and several residents reflected that employment at the Academy was the saving grace for many families, especially during the Great Depression.

Currently, Bancroft Hall, the dominant building on the campus, houses 4,000 midshipmen, officers, shops to provide needed services, and a dining room where all midshipmen are fed simultaneously three times daily. In 1976, the first women were admitted and now comprise 27 percent of the Brigade of Midshipmen.

The picturesque Naval Academy grounds contain a visitor's center, a cemetery, and several museums that illustrate the colorful history of the Navy. All of the buildings and sports fields are popular stops for tourists and families of the midshipmen. The crypt containing the remains of Captain John Paul Jones (1747-1792), born in Scotland and an emigrant to America, is considered the father of the United States Navy. The crypt is located in the lower level of the Navy Chapel. His remains were discovered in France and reinterred at the Naval Academy in 1913. John Paul Jones is remembered in the history books for his quote during a desperate battle with a British frigate off the northern coast of England during the American Revolution: "I have not yet begun to fight!" His courage and naval career are well documented. The green dome of the Naval Academy Chapel can be seen from miles away.

John Paul Jones shares this unofficial title of father of the United States Navy with a contemporary, Commodore John Barry (1745-1803). John Barry was born in Ireland and after emigrating to America joined the naval forces of the American Revolution. His naval exploits and courage are also well documented. John Barry is buried in Philadelphia's Old St. Mary's Churchyard. A statue of Commodore Barry stands in Independence Square.

Second President John Adams is also referred to as the "Father of the Navy" for establishing a naval department during his presidency (1797-1801). Adams is remembered for his attempts to protect shipping rights of the United States and efforts to keep the country out of the growing hostilities between France and England. France had formally allied with the Americans and entered the Revolutionary War in 1778. Marquis de Lafayette, with the aid of General Jean-Baptiste de Rochambeau, both of France, and America's George Washington and their troops fought until the surrender of British Lord General Charles Cornwallis' forces in Yorktown, Virginia, in 1781. The American Revolutionary War had ended after more than five years of fighting. King George III of the Royal House of Hanover who reigned from 1760-1820 had lost the American colonies, a big part of the British Empire. Only 31 years passed between England's surrender at Yorktown and the beginning of the next war with them in 1812. Unlucky George III, still on the throne of England, lost two wars with America (Revolutionary War and War of 1812). Eighty years after Yorktown, the American Civil War began. By then, Queen Victoria was on the throne of England. The United States Navy has continued its defense role in all American wars.

Source: www.navy.com;
www.history.com/topics/american-revolutionary/johnpauljones;
www.USHistory.org/people/commodorebarry.htm

The Parole Rotary Club contracts with the Naval Academy Athletic Association (NAAA) to direct traffic at all Navy football home games held at the Navy-Marine Corps Memorial Stadium. This work is part of Parole Rotary's community service commitment. Give a shout-out to the hard-working Parole Rotarians when you attend the games – you will know them by their bright gold hats with navy blue lettering, or navy blue with gold lettering. The Parole Rotary Club could always use some extra volunteers if you would like to be part of a fun day. And you will get to join us at our tailgate following the game too. Hope to see you there!

The Navy Hymn: "Eternal Father, Strong to Save"
The original words of the Navy Hymn were written as a poem in 1860 by William Whiting of Winchester, England, for a student leaving for the United States. Whiting was educated at Chapham and Winchester. He became master of Winchester College Choristers' School because of his musical ability. In addition to composing the Navy hymn, he also published two poetry collections.

The melody, published in 1861, was composed by fellow Englishman, Rev. John Bacchus Dykes, an Episcopalian clergyman. At the age of 10, young Dykes became the assistant organist at St. John's Church in Hull, where his grandfather was the vicar. He studied at Wakefield and St. Catherine's College, earning a B.A. in Classics in 1847. He co-founded the Cambridge University Musical Society and is best known for the over 300 hymn tunes that he composed.

In August of 1941, at the creation of the Atlantic Charter aboard the Royal Navy battleship HMS *Prince of Wales* docked in Newfoundland, and attended by President Roosevelt and Prime Minister Winston Churchill, the Navy Hymn was played, at Churchill's request. The eight declarations of the Atlantic Charter are available on-line.

The Navy Hymn was said to be 32nd President Franklin Roosevelt's favorite. He had been Secretary of the Navy early in his career. The Navy Hymn was sung at his funeral in Hyde Park, New York, in April of 1945; World War II had not yet ended. Germany surrendered 25 days after his death and Japan surrendered 4 months later.

The Navy Hymn was played by the Navy Band in 1963 as 35th President John F. Kennedy's coffin was carried up the steps of the U.S. Capitol to lie in state following his assassination in Dallas, Texas. Kennedy had commanded a Naval PT-109 boat in World War II in the Pacific Theater and suffered from his war injuries for the rest of his life following his actions to save his surviving crew after the boat under his command was sunk by a Japanese destroyer.

At the funerals of 37th President Richard Nixon (1994), 38th President Gerald Ford (2006), and 41st President George H.W. Bush (2018), the Navy Hymn was performed by the Naval Academy chorus. All three presidents had served heroically in the Navy during World War II in the Pacific Theater. The hymn was also sung at 40th President Ronald Reagan's funeral (2004).

In 2016, in memory of the 75th anniversary of the attack on Pearl Harbor in Hawaii and those who lost their lives in defense of our country, the Naval Academy chorus sang the Navy Hymn at the

USS Arizona Memorial. A video of the attack interspersed with the singing is available on line.

The Navy Hymn was sung by the congregation and choir during the funeral service for Arizona Senator John McCain (2018). He too suffered for the rest of his life from the injuries he sustained when the airplane he was piloting was shot down, his capture, and his nearly six-year brutal prisoner-of-war confinement during the Vietnam War. Senator McCain spent his entire career in service to his country. He is buried in the Naval Academy Cemetery, along with many other American patriots who served their country with distinction and honor.

The U.S. Naval Academy chorus often sings the Navy Hymn at military and patriotic events. Beautiful renditions are available on line, providing an opportunity for all to implore the Eternal Father to keep the men and women in service to our country safe at sea and on land.

Source: www.navy.com

Union Soldiers in Parole

From the earliest days of the Civil War, the North and South held a great number of prisoners. Although the federal government did not want to take any action that could be interpreted as recognizing the rebel states as a legitimate government, Secretary of War Edwin Stanton authorized the use of a Cartel that was in force during the War of 1812 as a basis for a prisoner exchange program.

On July 22, 1862, a Cartel was signed by Major General John A. Dix of the Union Army and Major General D. H. Hill of the Confederate Army, allowing for the exchange of prisoners. Union soldiers captured in the South by the Confederate Army were placed by the Confederacy on a Union ship and brought to Annapolis to be kept in a parole camp. They were designated as paroled soldiers. They could not participate in any military activities until they were released from the Parole Camp to return to their regiment.

Most paroled Union soldiers in the East were delivered by the Confederate Army to Aiken's Landing, and later City Point, on

Camp Parole Historical Sign
Image courtesy of Les Howard Studios

the James River in Virginia, placed on a Union "flag-of-truce-boat," and then taken to the St. John's College campus in Annapolis. There they were cleaned up, deloused, given a new uniform, and taken by train, or marched, to Camp Parole. They stayed in the Camp until the Union Army sent a captured Confederate soldier back to the Confederate Army to be placed in a parole camp in the South. Then a Union soldier in the Parole Camp would be allowed to go back to his regiment and an equal number of Confederate soldiers could go back to their Southern regiments.

The camp was originally in tents on the grounds of St. John's College, next to what is now called College Creek. The school buildings were used as hospitals. Because of the growing number of Union soldiers being exchanged and the rowdiness of soldiers with nothing but time on their hands, the camp was moved for a short period of time to a location on the south side of Forest Drive, between Greenbriar Lane and Bywater Road.

Finally, 250 acres were leased from Charles S. Welch for $125 per month. The buildings were built by the soldiers, and Camp Parole was established. Modern research places the camp north to south between West Street and Forest Drive and east to west between Chinquapin Round Road and Route 2. The camp complex consisted of 60 barracks, tents, large storehouses, 20 kitchens, 6 hospital buildings, and various administrative buildings, including a photography shop. Sutlers' buildings, which were places where civilian merchants sold provisions to the army, were also built. All were built around the camp.

Sergeant Lucius W. Barber, who served in Company D of the 15th Illinois Volunteer Infantry Regiment, was captured in Georgia. He spent time in the hell of Andersonville Prison, but was eventually put on a Confederate ship in Savannah Harbor to be taken to be exchanged. He recounts in his diary his first sight of Old Glory as they approached the Union ship: "I never saw a sight which awoke more innobling feelings of pride and elevation in my bosom than when I again beheld our noble ensign floating over our gallant ship which was soon to bear us back again to home and friends. Eyes that had long been straining to catch a glimpse of the dear old flag, now grew misty with tears. Yes, soldiers who had faced death time and time again with unfailing eyes, now wept like children before that flag that had so often guided them on to victory."

Sergeant Barber also described in his diary his arrival in Annapolis and his time in Camp Parole: "The ship anchored about midnight in the harbor of Annapolis. We disembarked at early dawn and marched to the barracks outside the city. It seemed pleasant to again get into God's country under the protection of the stars and stripes. Everyone seemed to vie in treating us kindly. In the evening we drew a complete suit of clothing, but before changing we were required to divest ourselves of every article of prison apparel, go into a bath room, prepared expressly for us, and thoroughly cleanse ourselves. We were also obliged to leave our prison apparel. Our new suit was furnished us free gratis. After our change our transformation was complete. We looked like a different set of beings.

"Arose early after a good night's rest. Ate breakfast and then marched to the parole camp, three miles south of the city. It was a splendid camp, well and tastefully arranged, laid out in regular streets, excellent barracks, warm and well ventilated, with cook houses, etc. The sanitary commission had an office on the ground and it proved a friend to the soldiers in time of need. Passed my first night in a parole camp and it proved pleasant and agreeable. Arose early, answered to roll-call and then took breakfast, which consisted of soft bread, boiled bacon or beef and coffee. For dinner we had bread and bean soup. The sanitary commission has been busy all day distributing needful articles amongst the prisoners, such as thread, paper, envelopes, combs, etc. A large sutler's stand is also on the ground. A large washhouse is nearby which contains fifty tubs and other accommodations for washing clothes. The whole camp presents a neat and wholesome appearance, the streets being wide and kept perfectly clean. This camp will accommodate ten thousand soldiers, with good hospitals for the sick. An order was read to us today that all paroled prisoners would receive thirty days furlough and two months pay as soon as the papers could be made out."

Religion played a part in the daily lives of many soldiers in the camp. As Bingham Findly Junkin of the 100th Pennsylvania Volunteer Infantry records in his diary, "Got aboard of a transport and had a very pleasant ride down the bay to Annapolis. March out about three miles to camp which gave us a good appetite for our hard tack. After supper some of the boys got to dancing and seemed to enjoy themselves right well. I step into a cookhouse and sit down by the stove and endeavored to cast my thoughts on God, ask him to take care of my dear ones at home, keep me and preserve me from evil. Oh, how much grace the Christian soldier needs and how comforting the thought that God reigns everywhere. Sabbath – spent the day pleasantly reading and having God's word. Attended Bible class in Chapel in camp parole near Annapolis at 11:00 o-clock. Heard Chaplain Dixon at 2 o-clock and a Rev. Moore of the Christian Communion at seven – he's from Massachusetts. Oh, how pleasant when separated from the endearment of home to enjoy such privileges. How good God is to thus provide for the instruction and comfort of his people under every circumstance."

Some of the boredom in waiting to be exchanged is contained in a letter Sergeant Francis Reed of the Pennsylvania Volunteers wrote to his family: "We arrived here yesterday morning, we heard that exchanging had been stopped. We are all very anxious to be exchanged to go back and square accounts with some of the rebels in the vicinity of Murfreesboro. We are entirely out of money. The rebels took all my clothes. They did not leave me anything except what I had on. I have no change and I am pretty dirty. If we do not get exchanged, I shall try and get a furlough from here for a few weeks. All are anxious to be exchanged, we have sent several petitions to Secretary Stanton asking to be exchanged, but no attention is paid to our petitions. I have wrote to the Captain to go to the General Commanding the Western Division to have us exchanged, but have received no answer yet. I only wish we could get out of this place. Never have I been so discouraged as since being here. Everyone is dissatisfied and all want to go home or be exchanged. So there is continual growling, we are comfortably quartered now, the boys will all have blankets and tomorrow they will all get a new suit from head to foot, we have plenty to eat and drink coffee twice a day, we have fresh bread every day, fresh beef three times a week, salt pork three times a week, bean soup three or four times a week and salt beef at any time, so we don't suffer for anything. We all have new clothes and look like soldiers again. George Fraser of Company K tried to leave camp on Wednesday last but was stopped, and is now in jail for mutiny in camp. He was going to take 100 men with him, and if my foot would not have been sore I should have made the attempt with him. We have not been paid yet but are promised from day to day. We know nothing about exchange, fifty different stories are raised daily. Our camp increases every day, we number about 4,000 men now."

Eventually the soldiers would be exchanged, but in late August of 1864, General Ulysses S. Grant suspended all parole and exchange of prisoners. Thousands upon thousands of Union soldiers released by the South, however, with no hope of exchange of Southern prisoners, continued to flow into Annapolis and Camp Parole. Prisoners continued to arrive until six weeks after the war ended. Most of them were in such bad condition they went immediately to one of the hospitals at the camp.

Clara Barton

One of the famous people who had an office at Camp Parole was Clara Barton, founder of the American Red Cross. There, she established the Office of Correspondence with Friends of the Missing Men of the United States Army with the endorsement of President Lincoln. Her task was to locate missing soldiers, and what better place to begin that job than where so many soldiers returned from the South as from the dead. She was able to determine the fate of about 22,000 men. For a time after the war ended, troops were stationed at Camp Parole to help maintain order in Anne Arundel County as men returned from the war.

Finally, all the buildings were torn down, some of the wood was sold, and some given to the Freedman's Bureau to help build houses in Parole for the newly freed slaves, the Mill Swamp School and the Stanton School (now Stanton Center) in Annapolis.

Nothing now remains of the camp but the memories of those who waited out their parole time and perhaps the ghosts of those who had fought the good fight and spent their last days in Camp Parole.

Source: Michael Roblyer, Rotarian and Attorney with offices in Parole

For More Information about Camp Parole

A Low, Dirty Place: The Parole Camps of Annapolis, Maryland (1862-1865) was written by R. Rebecca Morris in 2012 and published by the Ann Arrundell County Historical Society. An easily accessible online interview is available on line of the author discussing the book she wrote about Camp Parole (key in her name on line to view the video). She met with several book committee members to discuss her research at Maryland Archives and elsewhere. Her book can be purchased through Amazon. We recommend her work on the Parole camps to our readers.

President Abraham Lincoln in Annapolis via Parole

In February of 1865, President Abraham Lincoln, who was re-elected to a second term less than three months earlier, made a last-minute decision to attend what became known as the Hampton Roads Conference near Union-controlled Fort Monroe in Virginia. His Secretary of War, William Seward, was the only other negotiator representing the Union. The conference took place aboard the steamer *River Queen*.

Lincoln saw the trip as the best opportunity to set forth peace terms ending the Civil War. Because there was too much ice on the Potomac River, a decision was made for Lincoln to take the railroad to Annapolis, and then a steamer south on the Chesapeake Bay. He and one aide boarded the train in Washington and headed to Annapolis, transferring at Annapolis Junction to the Annapolis & Elk Ridge Railroad before arriving in Annapolis.

He would have been able to view the sprawling Camp Parole from the right side of the train five stops before the terminal in Annapolis.

Abraham Lincoln

He arrived at the Calvert and West Street station terminal around 1:00 p.m. on February 2 and walked the approximate one-half mile to the deep water port at the Naval Academy, probably on the rail line set down by General Benjamin Butler in 1861. On his left, he would have seen St. John's College, which was closed as an educational institution during the war and used instead as a hospital. He would also have walked near the State House, where the Maryland Senate was considering ratification of the Thirteenth Amendment to the Constitution ending slavery. He and the aide boarded a ship, the *Thomas Colyer*, and, avoiding ice in the Chesapeake Bay, arrived in Hampton late that night.

The next day the President and Secretary Seward met with the delegation from the Confederacy: Alexander Stephens, Vice President; Robert Hunter, Senator from Virginia; and John Campbell, Assistant Secretary of War and a Justice of the Supreme Court before the Civil War began. Campbell joined the Confederate cause after Lincoln's first inaugural address.

The conference went on for four to five hours, but no record was kept of the proceedings, by agreement. Many historians have written about the significance of the meeting. Participants wrote their own versions later, specifically the terms of peace to include complete surrender of the Confederacy, the end of slavery, and then rejoining the Union. There was also a discussion of prisoner-of-war exchanges.

Lincoln then left Hampton Roads and returned via the same route. President Lincoln's trip had been reported in the news, so a train met his boat at the Naval Academy, sparing him the long walk back through Annapolis. As far as we can determine, this trip was his only visit through Annapolis. He returned to the White House early that morning. The war dragged on for another two months.

Had Lincoln lived to write his memoirs, he might have shared his thoughts about seeing Camp Parole through the train windows, and whether seeing it entered into his discussions with the Confederates about prisoner-of-war exchanges. We will never know what effect seeing Camp Parole might have had on his thinking.

Source: www.History.com

For More Information about President Lincoln's Trip to Annapolis
Lincoln in Annapolis: February 1865 was written by Rockford Toews, owner of Annapolis book store Back Creek Books, and published by the Maryland State Archives.

Marylanders Benjamin Banneker and Frederick Douglass

These Marylanders are memorialized at the Banneker-Douglass Museum, 84 Franklin Street, Annapolis, Maryland, built on the foundation of the old Mt. Moriah African Methodist Episcopal (AME) Church.

Mount Moriah AME Church

The 2-1/2-story gabled, Gothic Revival style brick church, Mount Moriah AME Church, was constructed in 1875 and remodeled in 1896. The church lasted almost 100 years for worshipers in the Parole and Annapolis area. The building has been leased to the Maryland Commission on African-American History and Culture and serves as the state's official repository of African-American culture. It also houses a library, art gallery, and archives. When the building opened as the Banneker-Douglass Museum in 1984, an adjoining 2-1/2-story addition was added, which serves as the entrance to the museum. The church was saved by the Annapolis city preservation law, which the courts upheld when then Annapolis Mayor John Apostol wanted it demolished to expand the county courthouse. The church was listed on the National Register of Historic Places in 1973 and is located within the boundaries of the Colonial Annapolis Historic District, just off Church Circle in Annapolis.

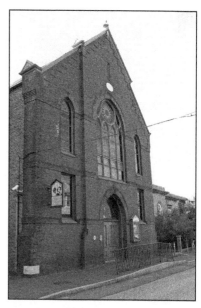

Banneker Douglas Museum
Image courtesy of Les Howard Studios

Benjamin Banneker

Benjamin Banneker (1731-1806) has a heritage with lots of twists and turns His grandmother, Molly Welsh, a white Englishwoman, arrived in America as a convicted felon for supposedly having stolen a bucket of milk, except that the cow apparently kicked over the bucket of milk. As was the custom, she was shipped to the New World and indentured for seven years to a tobacco plantation owner in Maryland who paid for her

Benjamin Banneker

passage. After seven years, she was released from her servant status and bought a 120-acre farm considered of negligible value near the Patapsco River, which is 39 miles long and flows from Baltimore into the Chesapeake Bay. Molly purchased two enslaved men from a ship in the Chesapeake Bay to help run the farm. She freed her slaves in 1696.

Although interracial marriages were prohibited by law, Welsh married one of her freed slaves, named Bannaky. They had four daughters before he died at a young age, and she was left to raise the children and manage the farm by growing, buying, and selling tobacco. Her eldest daughter Mary grew up and bought an enslaved man named Robert, who was from Guinea, West Africa. They bought his freedom. She later married him and they took the last name Banneky in honor of Mary's father. Over time, the spelling of Banneky became Banneker. Robert and Mary Banneker became Benjamin Banneker's parents. Since by law, free/slave status depended on the mother, Banneker, like his mother, was technically free.

Benjamin Banneker's early education was from his grandmother and from attendance at a nearby integrated Quaker school. An avid reader, he became proficient in astronomy, mathematics, and clockmaking. Banneker inherited his family farm when his parents died, and he continued growing tobacco, using sophisticated irrigation techniques. During the Revolutionary War, wheat grown on a farm designed by Banneker helped save the fledgling U.S. troops from starving. Banneker taught himself surveying. He also became an avid abolitionist.

Banneker became friends with George Ellicott (1760-1832), whose family ran the Ellicott Mills near where he lived in Howard County. An admirer of the five almanacs Banneker published was then Secretary of State Thomas Jefferson. In 1789, Banneker was called on to assist George Ellicott and Pierre Charles L'Enfant (1754-1825), the Frenchman George Washington had befriended during the Revolutionary War, in laying out what would become the nation's capital. It is believed that Washington's idea of what the new federal capital should look like was fashioned from his admiration for the layout of the city of Annapolis, with the capital as the centerpiece of all roads. After a year of work, L'Enfant stormed off the job, taking all the plans. Banneker, who had been placed on the planning committee at Thomas Jefferson's request, saved the project by reproducing from memory, in two days, a complete layout of the streets, parks, and major buildings. Thus Washington, D.C., itself can be considered a monument to this genius, known as the first African-American man of science. His writings contained the words, "Ah, why will men forget that they are brethren?" Banneker's likeness was portrayed on a U.S. stamp in 1980. Banneker died at the age of 75, 55 years before the beginning of the Civil War.

Frederick Douglass

The life of Frederick Douglass (1818-1895) began in Talbot County on the Eastern Shore of Maryland. He was the son of an enslaved woman and a white father. Upon his escape from slavery at the age of 20, he moved to Rochester, New York. One of his contemporaries and friends in Rochester was Susan B. Anthony, an activist for women's rights. Women could not own property or vote at the time. Douglass wrote three autobiographies, sometimes used as anti-slavery propaganda. His work as an abolitionist in the early 1840s drew the attention of Abraham Lincoln. For 16 years in Rochester, he edited the most influential black newspapers of the mid-19th century. Douglass achieved international fame as a fiery orator and writer who used his skills to indict slavery and racism, while providing a voice of hope for his people.

Douglass welcomed the Civil War as a moral crusade to eradicate slavery and worked for the Union cause and emancipation. On at least two occasions, he was an adviser to President Abraham Lincoln. Douglass recruited former enslaved and free men, including his two sons, into the Union Army. Douglass confronted

Frederick Douglass

the President in the White House to register his complaints about unequal wages for colored troops fighting for the Union and for lack of protection for those troops taken prisoner by the Confederacy. While not completely satisfied with the President's response, Douglass continued his recruiting to bring the war to an end. Douglass attended Lincoln's second inauguration and heard the President call slavery an offense against God. Douglass told the President that his inaugural speech was a sacred effort.

In the 1870s, Douglass moved his family to Washington, D.C. His home in the Anacostia neighborhood has been refurbished and preserved. It is known as the Frederick Douglass National Historic Site. His summer home in the Highland Beach community of Anne Arundel County, Maryland, fronting the Chesapeake Bay has also been preserved. It is now known as Twin Oaks, the Frederick Douglass Museum and Cultural Center. In Washington, Douglass edited *The New National Era* newspaper and served as Ambassador to Haiti. He crusaded against "Jim Crow" laws and other racial issues. His most popular lecture was the "Self-Made Man," first delivered in 1895, which became a reflection on his own life. Douglass had five children by his first wife Anna Murray, a free black woman from Baltimore who followed him out of slavery in 1838. After Anna died in 1882, the then 63-year old Douglass married Helen Pitts, his white former secretary, an event that created some controversy.

Douglass often referred to Maryland as his "own dear native soil." Douglass became a symbol of his age, a unique American voice for social justice, and the dilemma of being black in America. He died of heart failure at the age of 77, 30 years after the end of the Civil War.

Sources:

Banneker: *Federal Gazette* of Philadelphia obituary and his letters to Thomas Jefferson

Douglass: Autobiographies and correspondence

www.FDFI.org

Lecture of Kenneth Morris, Jr., great-great-great grandson of Frederick Douglass and great-great grandson of Booker T. Washington, at St. John's College, Annapolis, in commemoration of the 200th anniversary of Douglass' birth in 1818

Frederick Douglass Family Initiatives' reprint of "Narrative of the Life of Frederick Douglass,"

Artifacts of Banneker-Douglass Museum in Annapolis

Public Servants Representing Parole

William H. Butler, Sr., and William H. Butler, Jr.

William H. Butler, Sr. (circa 1829-1892) was probably born into slavery in Maryland, but was listed in Anne Arundel County Records as a free person of color. He was a carter (someone who transports a load on a cart drawn by a beast of burden), a carpenter, and one of the wealthiest free blacks in Annapolis during the 1860's. Butler married Sarah (or Sally) Brown who was born free in Annapolis, the daughter of William and Sarah (nee Shorter) Brown. Sarah Brown's maternal uncle, Charles Shorter, was a master carpenter who in 1838 built the first Asbury Methodist Church in Annapolis for a black congregation. Butler bought a house that still exists at 148 Duke of Gloucester Street in 1863 for $550. He donated two lots to the Maryland Colored Baptist Church, now the First Baptist Church on W. Washington Street off West Street, and row houses to rent. His civic commitment included building schools and churches, and he was one of the first trustees of Stanton School, one of Annapolis' earliest schools for black children. He was part of the thriving free black community and was involved with the Bishop, Price, and Shorter families. The Butlers had 12 children. His skills as a carpenter during the building boom in Annapolis in the 1860s and 1870s enabled him to also acquire real estate. Sarah Butler continued living in the house on Duke of Gloucester Street until she died, and the house remained in the family until 1922. Butler died a wealthy man and made provisions for their children.

In 1873, Butler was elected to serve on the Annapolis City Council, becoming the first African-American to be elected to state office in Maryland. He served for two years.

William H. Butler, Jr., his son, was a teacher at the Stanton Colored School and served on the Annapolis City Council from 1893 to 1897.

Thomas Norwood Brown
T. Norwood Brown (1912-1989) was born in Parole, was raised by his grandparents, and attended local schools. He was elected Alderman of the old 7th ward in 1950, making Annapolis the first city in Maryland to have three African-American aldermen serving on a city council. The other two were Dr. Oliver McNeill and Charles Oliver, both Republicans, like Brown. Brown was both a businessman and a community leader who owned the Arundel Cab Company. He was also serving as President of the Parole Improvement Association when elected alderman. He built the first Parole post office, located at 1979 West Street near Hicks Avenue, and became its postmaster. He advocated for the construction of the first YMCA in Parole. He built the Parole Confectionary at 1977 West Street, known as the "$50,000 Parole Drive-In." The food was excellent, according to locals. The building with its corner entrance still stands at the corner of West Street and Hicks Avenue. Brown was instrumental in having Parole annexed to the city in 1951, and served as its first alderman, remaining on the city council until 1967. When he resigned from the city council, John T. Chambers, Jr., took his place. Whatever was going on in the community, Brown was involved, a strong leader and a master at seeking compromise.

John T. Chambers, Jr.
John T. Chambers, Jr., (1928-2011) was the son of Rev. John T. Chambers, Sr., and Ruth Hicks Chambers. He grew up in Parole

on Hicks Avenue, named for his grandfather. After graduating from Bates High School and the Hampton Institute in Virginia and serving in the Korean War, John Chambers, Jr., served on the Annapolis City Council for 14 years, first as an appointee in 1967 representing Ward 7, and then in 1973, he ran for alderman in the newly formed Ward 3. His accomplishments included road and storm drain improvements, making the job of mayor a full-time position, and spelling out the duties of the mayor. Chambers advocated for the large African-American population in Ward 3 and succeeded in passing rent control, placing a plaque at City Dock in honor of Alex Haley's ancestor Kunta Kinte, and passing legislation making Martin Luther King, Jr.'s birthday a city holiday. He led the fight to save the Annapolis Youth Service Bureau, an organization created to prevent and decrease family disruption and juvenile delinquency. The Bureau was established in 1972 as part of the Anne Arundel County Community Action Agency and is housed in the Stanton Community Center. In 1981, Chambers was named Acting Mayor following the death of Mayor Gustav Akerland. Chambers' appointment made him the first African-American mayor of Annapolis. He served from April 12 to June 7, 1981. Following his retirement, he continued to work at his father's barber shop.

Samuel L. Gilmer
Samuel Gilmer (1922-2008) was born in North Carolina and moved to Baltimore as a four-year-old with his father after his mother's death. They later settled in Annapolis, where his father owned a grocery store and a taxi business. Gilmer was a 1940 graduate of Bates High School and attended the old Cortez Peters Business School in Baltimore. During World War II, he was a medical corpsman in France and Germany. After the war, he

attended George Washington University and worked at the Navy Ship Research Development Center and Montgomery Ward. He became active in the civil rights movement upon returning from World War II. He said after fighting against Hitler and Nazism, he resented coming home to a segregated country. Finding himself and other former black soldiers treated as second-class citizens in segregated states such as Maryland, he joined the fight for freedom and marched to get restaurants and hotels on the highways opened so blacks could enjoy the same things as everyone else. He organized the Anne Arundel Chapter of the National Association for the Advancement of Colored People (NAACP) and was its president in the 1960s and 1970s. Gilmer represented the 3rd Ward on the Annapolis City Council, beginning in 1981 and served for 20 years before being defeated in a primary. He died at 86. Many of his family members continue to live in Annapolis and Baltimore. The city of Annapolis later named the Department of Transportation complex on Chinquapin Round Road in his honor.

Source: www.Maryland.gov

Classie Gillis Hoyle

Classie Gillis Hoyle (b. 1936) was born in Annapolis. When she was three, her sister two, and her brother nine months old, their father died from appendicitis because he could not be treated at the Anne Arundel Hospital then located in downtown Annapolis, due to state and local segregation laws. Her mother and the three children moved to Baltimore to be with other family members. They had been living with an uncle in Annapolis who owned a house in Parole. She spent summers in Annapolis and remembers the ice wagons and vegetable trucks going through the neighborhoods. She went to college, got three degrees, married, and had children. When she moved back to the area in the 1960s she remodeled the house on Forest Drive and lived there until her most recent illness. Dr. Hoyle ran for Annapolis City Council in 2000 and served three terms before retiring in 2012. She advocated for residents of Parole and spearheaded the wording and placement of historical markers throughout Ward 3. It is her legacy to have the markers as reminders of what the shopping centers and condominiums have replaced. Annexation of Parole by the City of Annapolis brought paved roads, law enforcement, city water and sewer, natural gas lines, fire protection, and representation in city government. Dr. Hoyle worked with other city council members and community leaders in creating sidewalks, creating rules about including affordable housing in new developments and amending the city's charter so female members of the city council were called alderwomen, not aldermen.

Many of the streets in Parole are named for doctors who delivered babies at home because African-Americans were not allowed at the Anne Arundel Community Medical Center.

In 1909 the Maryland General Assembly disenfranchised black voters, thereby removing their right to vote. It took a ruling by the U. S. Supreme Court to restore the voting rights of African-Americans in the city of Annapolis in 1915. Representation of African-Americans changed as a result.

Rhonda Pindell Charles
Rhonda Pindell Charles, current Ward 3 alderwoman, replaced Dr. Classie Gillis Hoyle as the Ward 3 alderwoman in the city of Annapolis in 2013. She and her family have lived in the Parole community for several generations. She attended Parole Elementary, Annapolis Junior, and Annapolis Senior High schools.

She graduated from Morgan State University in 1976 with a major in Business Administration and a minor in Economics and then graduated from the University of Maryland School of Law in 1979. From then until 1983, she served as an attorney in the Maryland Attorney General's Office, Department of Natural Resources. After 20 years, she retired as an Assistant State's Attorney in Baltimore. She is married and has raised two children, all in Parole.

Alderwoman Pindell Charles' revised platform to continue her service on the city council is listed below. Comprehending the vastness of that platform and its ramifications for those she represents in Annapolis is a tall order for any leader.

1. Health and Public Safety
2. Balanced and Managed Growth and Development
3. Educational, Career, and Housing Opportunities
4. Business Community Initiatives; and Civic Engagement

Sources: Maryland Archives; Interviews with Alderwomen Classie Hoyle and Rhonda Pindell Charles by Joyce Edelson

Railroads into Annapolis and Camp Parole

Some form of passenger and freight railroad service was available from Washington, D.C., and Baltimore into Annapolis from 1840 to 1935. The lines serving Annapolis went through several name changes, originally called the Annapolis and Elk Ridge Railroad. Around 1870, it became the Annapolis and Elkridge Railroad Company (AE&R). Later it became the Washington, Baltimore and Annapolis (WB&A) and finally the Baltimore and Ohio (B&O). Three separate lines operated between Washington and Baltimore, the B&O, the Pennsylvania Railroad (the "Pennsy") and the Washington, Baltimore & Annapolis Electric Railroad (WB&A).

When traveling from Annapolis to either Washington or Baltimore, passengers had to transfer at Annapolis Junction near Odenton. In Washington, a passenger would get on at the then B&O station located at New Jersey Avenue and C Street, N.W. Several other stations existed in Washington until the world-famous Union Station was built in 1907. Many people moved to the Parole and Annapolis area because of access to railroad transportation. Parts of the old railroad lines still exist in Annapolis and Anne Arundel County as bicycle paths and rights of way.

Having railroads was important to the development of the area, both for passenger and freight purposes. The site for the third prisoner-of-war exchange camp in the area, Camp Parole, was chosen for its proximity to the railroad line. During the Depression of the 1930s, the advent of other means of transportation from railroads to buses and automobiles created the demise of the railroads and their tracks.

Historical Note: *On June 5, 1908, two of WB&A's single-car trains collided at Camp Parole, Maryland. As a result of the crash, nine people died. The trains were bringing riders to the Naval Academy for graduation ceremonies.*

Source: Maryland Archives

Parole Churches

As many citizens of Parole have reflected, the churches were the backbone and center of the community. They continue providing that spiritual sustenance. Churches located in the greater Parole area of Annapolis are listed as follows.

King's Apostle: 11 Kirby Avenue, Rev. Wilbert L. Baltimore

King's Apostle
Image courtesy of Les Howard Studios

Cecil Memorial
United Methodist Church
Image courtesy of Les Howard Studios

Cecil Memorial United Methodist Church: 15 Parole Street, Rev. Patricia A. Turnange. The following words appear on the plaque shown in the picture of the church: "This church was founded on July 16, 1925, by Rev. John C. Cecil, a retired minister of the former Washington Conference and member of the Asbury Quarterly Conference of Annapolis. His wife, Annie B. Cecil, was a great supporter of his effort. This church was originally named Asbury United Methodist Episcopal Church."

Mt. Olive A.M.E Church
Image courtesy of Les Howard Studios

Mt. Olive A.M.E. Church: 2 Hicks Avenue, Rev. Johnny Calhoun. The church was founded in 1870 as Macedonia A.M.E. Church, having been built at another location in 1952; the current church replaced the frame structure built in the 1880s.

Beacon Light Seventh Day Adventist Church: 1943 Drew Street, Pastor Claude Harris II

Beacon Light Seventh Day Adventist Church
Image courtesy of Les Howard Studios

Capital Church of Christ
Image courtesy of Les Howard Studios

Capital Church of Christ: 1790 Lincoln Drive, Rev. Douglas Goodman

Asbury United Methodist Church: 87 West Street, Rev. Dr. Carletta Allen. This church is the oldest African-American church in Annapolis and Anne Arundel County.

Asbury United Methodist Church
Image courtesy of Les Howard Studios

Mt. Moriah AME Church
Image courtesy of Les Howard Studios

Mt. Moriah AME Church: 2204 Bay Ridge Avenue, Sister Valerie Bell

Bridge Church: 207 Chinquapin Round Road

Bridge Church
Image courtesy of Les Howard Studios

First Baptist Church: 31 West Washington Street, Rev. Louis Boston

First Baptist Church
Image courtesy of Les Howard Studios

Second Baptist Church: 1808 Poplar Avenue (originally on West side of Larkin Street)

Second Baptist Church
Image courtesy of Les Howard Studios

Trinity United Methodist Church: 1300 West Street, Pastor Chris Owens

Trinity United Methodist Church
Image courtesy of Les Howard Studios

Kingdom of Life Ministries: A church on the move, Pastor Rodney E. Simms; website: www.KLIMinistries.org

Source: Cecil Memorial United Methodist Church provided by Terrence Wright [Internet and telephone directories]

Parole Schools

Stanton School, the first so-called "colored" school, was built in 1867 in Parole and named after President Lincoln's Secretary of War Edwin Stanton. Wood from the recently evacuated Camp Parole barracks was used to build the initial structure on Washington Street. It was built by the Freedman's Bureau, the federal agency created to help newly freed people. At the turn of the century, a brick building replaced the wooden structure. It was first used as an elementary school, and then as the first high school for African Americans in Anne Arundel County. It remained in use as a school until the desegregation of the Anne Arundel County school system in 1966. The building then became a community center.

Stanton Center
Image courtesy of
Les Howard Studios

The Little Red Schoolhouse, the first elementary school in Parole, was located at the corner of West Street and Route 2, where the Double T Diner is now located. There do not appear to be any pictures of the school available, but many residents recall their parents and grandparents talking about their early schooling here.

Parole Elementary Rosenwald School. Julius Rosenwald (1862-1932), the son of first-generation German Jewish immigrants, built Sears, Roebuck & Co. into a famous mail-order and retail store. He teamed up with Educator Booker T. Washington, who built Tuskegee Institute in Alabama, and together they built more than 5,000 Rosenwald schools in 15 states in the rural south from 1917 through the early 1930's. All were funded by Rosenwald. There were 156 Rosenwald schools built in Maryland, 53 of which remain; there were 23 built in Anne Arundel County, 10 of which survive. The Rosenwald Elementary School, built in Parole in 1924-1925, still stands at the corner of Hicks Avenue and Dorsey Street. It has evolved into apartments. Avina Kempner has created a documentary, *Rosenwald*, available on line in DVD form. Until 1914, Maryland's only African American high school was located in Baltimore.

Parole Rosenwald School
Image courtesy of Les Howard Studios

Wiley H. Bates High School, completed in 1932, replaced the original Annapolis Colored High School. It was named after the prominent African-American businessman and community leader, Wiley H. Bates, whose financial donations built the school. Many additions followed. The building continued as a high school until the late 1960s when it became Bates Junior High school,

Former Bates High School, then Bates Junior High School, now Legacy Center
Image courtesy of Les Howard Studios

Maryland Hall, formerly Annapolis High School
Image courtesy of Les Howard Studios

which subsequently closed in 1981. It then reopened as Bates Middle School on Chase Street, near the vacated building of Annapolis High School, now Maryland Hall for the Creative Arts. Annapolis' new high school was built on Riva Road. Prior to desegregation in 1966, Bates was the only public school in the county that African-American students could attend for a secondary-level education. The site has been repurposed into 71 senior housing units, a senior center, a boys' and girls' club, and a Legacy Center Museum dedicated to Bates.

Wiley H. Bates

Walter S. Mills-Parole Elementary School is named after African-American educator Walter S. Mills (1909-1994) who was a teacher and then principal of Parole Elementary School. Mills advocated fiercely for his fellow teachers and equipment for his schools. When he asked George Fox, who had become the superintendent of the Anne Arundel County school system in 1916, for desks and chairs for his school, he was told to see if the then Finkelstein Junk Shop might have some desks for him. The answer was met with rather stiff resistance from Mills, according

Walter S. Mills–Parole Elementary School
Image courtesy of Les Howard Studios

to several fellow citizens of Parole, and soon Mills had new desks and chairs for his school.

Bates and Mills left a legacy of inspiration to the people of Parole, to the state of Maryland, and to the rest of the country.

Legal, Historical, and Constitutional Issues Involving Education and Civil Rights

In 1939 Walter S. Mills filed a lawsuit against the Anne Arundel County Board of Education that resulted in equal pay for black principals and teachers. At the time of the suit, white school principals received $1,800 a year, compared with the $1,050 that Mills and other black principals earned. Mills was the only plaintiff in the case and was represented by Marylander Thurgood Marshall, then a lawyer with the NAACP. Marshall argued that the salary discrepancy was caused by racial differences and violated the Equal Protection Clause of the 14th Amendment to the U.S. Constitution, which required equal protection of the law to all U.S. citizens and was ratified July 9, 1868. The school board tried to head off the legal action by offering Mills a 10-percent pay increase, but he refused the offer. The trial was acrimonious and manifested some of the worst instincts in local leaders. On January 12, 1940, Judge W. Calvin Chestnut of the U.S. District Court in Baltimore ruled in Mills' favor and in the decree "perpetually enjoined the School Board from discriminating in payment of salaries against the plaintiff and other colored teachers in the county." The

Walter Mills

Thurgood Marshall Statue
Lawyers Mall, Annapolis State House Grounds
Image courtesy of Les Howard Studios

case, *Mills v. Board of Education of Anne Arundel County*, is only one of two cited in law books concerning discriminatory pay practices in education. It came 15 years before the 1954 landmark case *Brown v. Board of Education of Topeka* case (see below). Mills had taught in St. Mary's and Charles Counties before coming to Parole Elementary School, where he spent 46 years before retiring in 1978. Mills also helped establish the Parole Health Center on Drew Street, still in operation and now a historical landmark.

Thurgood Marshall also argued the *Brown v. Board of Education of Topeka* case before the Supreme Court in 1954, which declared state laws establishing separate public schools for black and white students to be unconstitutional. The unanimous decision by the Supreme Court overturned the 1896 case that had arisen in New Orleans which allowed for "separate but equal" accommodations on railroad cars. That decision, *Plessy v. Ferguson* provided the legal foundation for the system of racial inequality known as "Jim Crow" (a derisive term for a black man) to segregate all public facilities, including schools. Additional "Jim Crow" legislation enforcing racial segregation in the southern and other states, including Maryland, held for 58 years before being overturned. Thirteen years after the Brown case, President Lyndon B. Johnson appointed Thurgood Marshall to the U.S. Supreme Court. He was the first African-American to serve as an Associate Justice of the Supreme Court and served for 24 years, until 1991. Of the 32 cases Marshall had previously argued before the Supreme Court, he won 29. His statue is located on Lawyer's Mall in front of the state capital in Annapolis.

Easily readable versions (with educational highlights) of the U.S. Constitution, including the Bill of Rights (first ten Amendments) and the additional 17 Amendments, are available on line. Of particular interest to the history of Parole are the 13th Amendment outlawing slavery and ratified December 6, 1865, the 14th Amendment requiring equal protection of the law to all U.S. citizens and ratified July 9, 1868, and the 15th Amendment guaranteeing the right of all citizens to vote regardless of race, color, or previous condition of servitude and ratified February 3, 1870. It took another 50 years before the 19th Amendment guaranteeing women the right to vote was ratified on August 18, 1920. The 24th Amendment eliminating the poll tax or other tax as a condition of voting was ratified January 23, 1964.

The Civil Rights Act of 1964 ended segregation in public places, provided for the integration of schools and other public facilities, and banned employment discrimination on the basis of race, color, religion, sex or national origin. The law was signed by 36th President Lyndon B. Johnson on July 2, 1964. The civil rights movement had begun in the mid-1950s and continued well after the 1964 Civil Rights Act was signed into law, beginning with the strategy known as massive resistance, declared by U.S. Senator Harry F. Byrd, Sr., of Virginia. The courageous fight to provide civil rights for all persons in America continues through the work of numerous individuals and organizations.

It was 400 years ago in 1619 that the first slaves were brought to Jamestown, Virginia. The institution and bondage of slaves in the United States continued until 1865 and the end of the Civil War 246 years later. The non-profit organization Worldwide Freedom estimates that more than 40 million persons throughout the world currently endure some kind of slavery. The United Nations Universal Declaration of Human Rights adopted in 1948, more than 70 years ago, outlined the 30 rights and freedoms every person should have. Through legislation and the courts, the United States and other countries have expanded rights of their citizens, some of which have been and continue to be subject to legal challenges. Many clubs of Rotary have programs dealing with human rights. An example is the Rotary Adventures and Human Rights Program in Winnipeg, Canada. Rotary history and human rights articles can be found on line.

Sources:
Maryland Archives
Plessy v. Ferguson, 163 U.S. 537 (1896)
Mills v. Board of Education of Anne Arundel County, 30 F. Supp. 245 (D. Md. 1939)
Brown v. Board of Education of Topeka, 347 U.S. 483 (1954)
U. S. Constitution

The Civil Rights Act of 1964, Pub. L. 88-352, 78 Stat. 241 (1964)

For More Information on Parole Schools

A Century of "Separate but Equal" Education in Anne Arundel County, a book written by the late Philip L. Brown, second printing in 2002, provides a well-researched history of Maryland schools and contains transcripts of the legal cases mentioned above, as well as other legal documents.

The Other Annapolis (Maryland) 1900-1950, is another book written by Philip L Brown, who was born in Annapolis and educated in Maryland public schools, Morgan College, and New York University, where he received his M.A. He taught in Anne Arundel County for 42 consecutive years. We commend his work to our readers. His books are available for purchase through Amazon.

Parole Cemeteries

Luther A. Palmer Memorial Cemetery, also known as Edwards Methodist Episcopal Chapel Cemetery, is in a triangle island where Riva Road meets West Street. Anne Arundel County developed roads on all three sides of the cemetery to handle traffic congestion. The cemetery is named after Luther Palmer, a local businessman who sold the parcel in 1897 to what was then the Edwards Methodist Chapel. The church sold its property to a motel chain and moved farther south on Riva Road, and renamed itself St. Andrews. It is currently associated with St. Andrews United Methodist Church in the Gingerville community of Edgewater. Among the names in the cemetery are Tilghman, Reynolds, and Palmer. The remaining tombstones, ranging from 1897 to 1978, include WWI and WWII veterans.

Luther A. Palmer Memorial Cemetery
Image courtesy of Les Howard Studios

St. Demetrios Greek Orthodox Cemetery
Image courtesy of Les Howard Studios

St. Demetrios Greek Orthodox Cemetery is next to the Annapolis Towne Center at Parole, with an entrance on Riva Road, just south of West Street behind the small hotel that faces the entrance of the Mission BBQ restaurant. The Towne Center was built around the cemetery.

Hillcrest Memorial Cemetery and Mausoleum
Image courtesy of Les Howard Studios

Hillcrest Memorial Cemetery and Mausoleum is located at 1911 Forest Drive, near Chinquapin Round Road, across from the Gardner Center.

Annapolis National Cemetery, 800 West Street near Westgate Circle at Taylor Avenue, Spa Road and West Street, is one of 14 national cemeteries that date from the Civil War. It is the final resting place for many Union soldiers who died in the nearby parole camp and hospitals. Some died of battlefield injuries, others of diseases that spread through the camps. In addition to white Union soldiers, soldiers of the U.S. Colored Troop Regiments, hospital nurses, at least 24 Confederate POW's who died in captivity, and one Russian sailor who died in Annapolis during the Civil war, are buried here. What

Annapolis National Cemetery
Image courtesy of Les Howard Studios

began as a private cemetery known as Ash Grove would later become the Annapolis National Cemetery. The cemetery officially closed to new internments in 1961. Today it contains nearly 3,000 graves in 15 burial sections spread over 4 acres. A portion of the original late 19th-century rubble-stone wall still stands, marking the cemetery's perimeter. Dating from 1940, the classical revival style entry gate is wide enough to accommodate automobiles. The current superintendent's lodge dates from the same year and replaced the original 1871 lodge. Constructed on the old foundation, the lodge is a brick Colonial Revival style building with a steeply pitched gable roof. Near the lodge are the cemetery's flagpole and two brick-and-concrete storage and utility buildings from 1936. Many soldiers buried here had no identification when they arrived at the Camp Parole railroad station. Often they were so ill and emaciated, that they did not make it to the camp hospitals. After the war, others were disinterred and their remains taken to their respective home cemeteries by their families.

Brewer Hill Cemetery is located on West Street, just west of Annapolis National Cemetery. The land once housed a Revolutionary War military hospital, was used for a smallpox hospital, and was also used as a pauper's cemetery. This was the first "colored" cemetery in Annapolis. From the beginning of slavery in this country, enslaved men, women, and children were buried here. The oldest marker found is dated 1789. In 1863, the same year as the Emancipation Proclamation issued by President Lincoln, 11 black Annapolis businessmen created the 4.5-acre cemetery from property owned by State Circuit Court Judge Nicholas Brewer that they purchased for $758. The judge died a year later, but his name was kept on the front gate. The late Annapolitan George Phelps' great-uncle William was one of the businessmen. He paid on the property for 35 years until it was paid off.

Brewer Hill Cemetery
Image courtesy of Les Howard Studios

Among others buried in Brewer Cemetery are educator Wiley H. Bates, Dr. William Bishop, who founded Anne Arundel General Hospital, and many other distinguished Annapolitans. Soldiers from the Civil War, the Spanish-American War, both world wars, and the Korean War are buried in the cemetery. It was not until 1942 that black soldiers were allowed burial in the National Cemetery next door. Restoration and maintenance of the cemetery continues by descendants of those buried there, along with other volunteers.

St. Mary's Cemetery, located across West Street from Brewer Hill Cemetery and assembled over 43 years from four parcels of land, was the first lot with a consecrated Catholic burial ground. The remaining acreage has always been open to lay Catholics and non-Catholics.

St. Mary's Cemetery
Image courtesy of Les Howard Studios

Sources: *Maryland Archives*
Cemetery websites

Memories of Parole

Katherine Joyce

Katherine Joyce, now in her 90s, grew up and lived much of her life in Parole. She remembers the post office and Camp Parole train station across from the Finkelstein store, the gypsies coming to the area, and visits from the Ku Klux Klan, the white supremacist organization formed in 1865 that employed intimidation, destruction of property, assault, and murder to achieve its aims and influence elections. She remembers her parents telling her the stories of local black men being lynched during their generation. The children walked to the Parole Elementary and Bates High schools, some from as far away as the South River. She went to nursing school in Baltimore and worked at the Public Health Hospital there, then went to cosmetology school and worked in that field for 45 years back in Parole. Babies of black mothers could not be born at the hospital, only at home until a maternity ward on Northwest Street became available. Doctors made house calls, and many babies were delivered at home. She is the only remaining family member of 13. She has four children and many grandchildren and great-grandchildren. Everybody raised and preserved their own vegetables, canned fruit from their fruit trees, gathered eggs from the chickens, and butchered hogs for pork and ham. Most were fairly self-sufficient. Produce that was not used for the family was sold to the canning factory on the northern side of the railroad. The canning factory and Naval Academy were the best sources of jobs. There were some stores in the neighborhood for food basics. She remembers going to Suzy's Tea Room and Gray's Crab Cake Shop. Other black businesses were Holt's Barbershop, the Service Center Barbershop, Charlene Marie's House of Beauty, Day's Vegetables, the Park Lunch, Carroll Hynson's real estate office, and more. Families are not as close as when she grew up. She has good memories. She does not dwell on what happened in the past, but simply moved on. She feels she had a good life and thanks God for it. She is surprised at the way Parole has changed with all the new high-rise buildings.

Pearl Swann

Pearl Swann, aunt to Alderwoman Rhonda Pindell Charles and also in her 90s, grew up on West Street and Poplar Street on the other side of the railroad tracks and has lived much of her life in Parole. She had three brothers and was the only girl in her family. Her father worked on the railroad, and her mother was a homemaker. They put cardboard inside their shoes to keep their feet warm. There were no buses for black students, and children from the whole county came to Bates High School. Finally one man with a bus began bringing the children from the county to school. Anne Arundel County Schools were not integrated until 1966. Church was the center of their lives, often going all day and evening on Sundays. She is very proud of her children: Her son is a minister, and her daughter worked as a principal in the school system. The main issue facing Parole during her lifetime was lack of affordable housing. She does not hold any malice about the past. Her husband worked at the Naval Academy. She worked at Britt's Department Store for 15 years in the Parole Plaza Shopping Center. Things were particularly hard in the Depression. Any jobs available rarely went to blacks, even though they could do the work. Most cut their own wood to heat their houses. Everyone sewed a lot; they had to make all their own clothes, because they could not afford to buy them. Crocheting was a favorite hobby for the ladies, and the men loved horseshoes. They had Boy Scouts and generations of champion basketball teams in the schools. She remembers Miss

Jones' kindergarten, and when the roads in the neighborhood were finally paved over dirt. Sidewalks came fairly recently. She is the last survivor of her immediate family and has grandchildren and great-grandchildren.

Alma Wright Cropper

Alma Wright's extended family lived across West Street from the AME church on Hicks Avenue, and near the Harlem Beer Garden. Her maternal grandfather, John Wesley Chambers, and grandmother, Susie Stepney, owned a farm on the property where the Life Center, behind the AME church, is now located. She helped pick the vegetables and fruit, which her grandfather sold all over the city, and gathered the eggs from the barn. The horse and buggy were kept in the barn, along with the pigs and chickens. They kept the potatoes and root vegetables in their cellar. In the fall, a slaughter day was held when the men in the community slaughtered their pigs and smoked the meat in their smokehouses behind their homes. The canned garden produce was kept in another room at the back of the smokehouse building. In the summer they cooked outside and ate in the house. Her grandfather was also custodian of the older church, made of wood and cardboard and heated with a pot-bellied stove. Singing and praying time was in July. She remembers her mother pointing out where the Little Red Schoolhouse she attended was located. Her father, Charles Wright, came from Havre De Grace and met Cropper's mother, Katrina Chambers, through a friend. He worked at Carvel Hall (the old Paca House, no longer in existence) and the Naval Academy. When she was a child, she was burned and taken to the segregated hospital on Cathedral Street. Her mother rubbed her burned face with cocoa butter and hogs' lard every day to heal the scars. She and her four siblings attended the Rosenwald School in Parole through sixth grade and then graduated from Bates School. She chose the Bates "vo-tech" curriculum run by Miss Nunley. She said they learned everything they needed to get through life. Her father died when she was seven. Her mother continued raising their five children while still working outside the home. Since there was no money for college, Cropper went to work at 16 at Carvel Hall waiting tables and later worked at Crownsville Hospital. Following that, she did home nursing and also worked as a clerk at Lipman's Dress Shop on Main Street, next door to Snyder's shoe store. She hurt her back and had to go on disability in the 1970s. Her sister Alice and three of her four children survive and live locally, along with five grandsons and five granddaughters. Her husband was Roland Cropper.

All of the Chambers property where her grandparents' farm was located was sold to the AME church. Rev. Johnny Calhoun, pastor of the AME church, and other community leaders negotiated with the new Parole Towne Center owners to build the Life Center for the people of Parole, as so much of what had long been a part of Parole, including the race track, had been transformed into highrises. Before the Life Center was built, the University of Maryland did a "big dig" on the property. Artifacts recovered from the property are located in a case at the Life Center.

Mount Olive Community Life Center
Image courtesy of Les Howard Studios

Bess Demas: Open Gate Restaurant and Hotel

Bess Demas shared her memories of Parole. Her parents were

Open Gate Restaurant

Greek immigrants: Theodore (Ted) and Mary Demas who came to America from Trikala, Thessaly, Greece. The Demas family first ran the Boston Dairy Luncheon on West Washington Street while Bess was an infant, and the family lived in an apartment above the restaurant while saving money to build a new restaurant in Parole. The family moved to Murray Avenue upon leaving West Washington Street. The name was changed to Victory Lunch by its new owners, the Samaras family.

In 1946, Ted and Mary Demas acquired property in Parole from Wilfred Azar. When asked why he would want to build way out in Parole, Demas said he thought that area was going to be the future of Annapolis, and he believed in the "go west, young man" motto. It took three years to build the Open Gate Drive-In Restaurant and Hotel, located at 2063 West Street Extended, Annapolis. Capital One Bank currently occupies that space. He partnered with first cousin John, or J., Charas. The building had a large key sign in front to symbolize the open gate. An alleyway was built to access their restaurant and a tobacco and vegetable farm owned by Mr. Mandris who rented it to a family. The alleyway was built on a handshake and $1 exchange. The alleyway was also shared by Delpar Corporation and a gas station next door.

Bess Demas and her sister often played with farmer's daughter Georgiana, who taught them about nature and farm living, such as gathering eggs from the hen house. The farm was surrounded by wildflowers and plants and a wooded area. They could walk through the fields to the harness racing track, owned by "Mush" Snyder of Snyder's Bootery in downtown Annapolis. One farmer left the tobacco and vegetable farm and another was hired, a man named Parker and his wife Ola May. He managed Taubman's Hardware Store downtown during the day and worked the farm at night. Ola May Parker was up at 4:30 to make breakfast for the farmhands, and then did the same for lunch. Sometime later they left the farm because it was getting too hard for them.

Mandris gave the farm to his niece by marriage, Helen Lewnes, who wanted to sell the property because her kids were growing up. Ted and Mary Demas bought it so other potential competition could not take away their restaurant business. Soft-shell crab sandwiches and hamburgers were specialties. Bess Demas' favorite pies were chocolate cream and French apple. The restaurant was the first in Annapolis to offer curb service, which they had to stop because the waitresses who brought the trays out sometimes forgot to collect the money. Cuccia's Oldsmobile dealership was next door to the restaurant. They shared parking. The inside of the restaurant had a pink and maroon motif. The family kept the restaurant until 1969. After the death of her father, Bess Demas, her sister, and her mother worked the restaurant and hotel rooms for about four years. An outdoor theater was built behind the restaurant once the harness racing track was removed. Demas wants her memories and heritage preserved as part of her family's legacy.

Dave Finkelstein and Ron and Marilyn Snyder: Finkelstein's to Snyder's Antiques to Return to Oz

The Finkelstein building, 2011 West Street in Parole, was built in 1916, at the corner of West and Old Solomon's Island Road, directly across the street from the Camp Parole railroad station.

This building has been both a house and a business, sometimes both. The original business had gas pumps in front, a general store inside, and living quarters upstairs and in the back. The extended Finkelstein family included some born in Russia and some in Baltimore. The bar in the front room from the 1930s and the trap door near the front door held colas and other liquids to keep them cold. In 1917, teenager Sam Finkelstein, who had come to America from Russia at the age of four not knowing a word of English, helped his mother open the store. Down the street, across from what is now McDonald's, was a grocery store owned and operated by Sam's father. Between the two stores, the Finkelstein family dominated the road between Annapolis and Parole. Finkelstein's became an institution and must-see place in Annapolis. In the 1940s the store became a bric-a-brac store, no doubt occasioned by the opening of an A&P grocery store in the neighborhood. In 1956, when West Street was widened, the house was moved 17 feet back on the property.

Finkelstein House / Business
Image courtesy of Les Howard Studios

Ron and Marilyn Snyder bought the property at 2011 West Street from Sam Finkelstein in 1984 and opened Snyder's Antiques. The retail store next door was built in the 1960s, and the Snyders leased that additional space. By then, the four-digit telephone number had changed to seven digits. They ran a successful antique operation a total of 23 years. The Snyders had run several businesses in the city prior to 1984. He tended the triangular flower garden at the corner of where Old Solomon's Island Road forks either right or left onto West Street until the city paved it and made room for a sidewalk in the middle. The Snyders won the golden trash award for having the cleanest and best looking place in the city, which meant they were able to display the gold trash cans for a month. They received the award a second time, after which the city did not give the award. The Snyders closed their shop in August of 2007 and are enjoying a well-deserved retirement in the area. They leased the space to Return to Oz, a fun and affordable second-hand business on both floors.

One of Sam Finkelstein's nephews, Dave Finkelstein, son of Milton and Bea, is one of the fourth (of six) generations of Finkelsteins still living in the area. In 1958, Dave Finkelstein's parents had moved from Cathedral Street to a house still standing at the corner of Poplar and N. Cherry Grove streets, across from the original Germantown School. His parents operated a grocery store in the neighborhood for 11 years, from 1955 to 1966. When Finkelstein was 17 and his sister 12, his father was killed in the store. His mother died in 1985, nine years after his father. His sister moved to Omaha. He has two daughters, one of whom lives in Annapolis, and two grandchildren. Finkelstein currently runs Bagels And... in a small strip mall at 2019 West Street in the building that had previously housed the A&P grocery store. Bagels And... is within shouting distance of his Uncle Sam's original Finkelstein's store. Just across the street what was a roller skating rink (when Finkelstein was growing up) became a Western Auto and is now Fiat. Colonial Bowling Lanes was down a bit across the street. Finkelstein mused that it was fun growing up in Annapolis. In 1964, Bates High School on Smithville Road merged with Annapolis High School (now Maryland Hall). He is carrying on the Finkelstein entrepreneurial spirit of his family. His lease will end in 2023. There no doubt will be plenty of delicious bagels available until then.

On the other property in this trio of buildings at 2007 West Street stood one of the first built and oldest homes in Parole, according to studies by students in the local school system. It was owned by Anne B. Cecil and used at different times as a rooming house. The current brick building extends far to the back. Many people had moved to the Parole area for job opportunities and accessibility to shopping centers. Some residents were employed by the U.S. Naval Academy and some at the gardening and canning factory across the railroad tracks on the other side of West Street. Horse and buggy was the transportation mode for those who were fortunate enough to have space and funds for the buggy, the horses, and feed for the animals. Having the Annapolis, Baltimore, and Washington steam train across the street (the Camp Parole station) was a plus. Riders could transfer at Annapolis Junction near Odenton to trains that would transport them to either Baltimore or Washington. When the railroad stopped running to Annapolis in the 1930s, buses became popular, the Red Star to Baltimore and the Greyhound to Washington. Taxis and autos also began filling in the transportation needs of the day.

Lorna Cunningham: Shady Oaks Inn

This property was located in Parole where Kohl's, Shoppers Food Warehouse, and Office Depot are now located (11+ acres total). That part of Forest Drive separating Shoppers and Office Depot was part of the property before it became a road. The

Shady Oaks Inn

Wagner family of several generations operated the property from the 1940s until the 1960s as the inn, cabins, trailer park, camping facilities, bus parking, stores, restaurants, a trading post, Tubby's ice-cream store, a bait store, a gas station, and Owen Basil's meat market.

Lorna Cunningham, who was born and grew up there, shared memories of her childhood. Her grandparents who came from Germany, built and ran the inn. It was also a boarding house, catering to parents of midshipmen, legislators, tourists, seasonal workers, and anyone who needed a place to stay and get some good food. Her grandmother was famous for her cooking. Her parents, Clem and Sweetie Wagner, and her brother, David, lived in a little house behind the inn (the phone number was 780W: three digits and one letter). In the summers, Cunningham ran a sno-cone stand. The children played in the ravine behind the former Colonial drive-in theater (where Home Depot is now), and found arrowheads and hand-made bullets probably left over from Camp Parole.

The race track owned by the Parole Hunt Club was still in the area, and the children ran their go-carts on the tracks. When the circus came to town, Cunningham learned tightrope walking and other circus tricks. She remembers playing with the monkeys. When gypsies came north during the summers in their Airstream trailers (some with chandeliers), the men went to work in various trades, such as building the Bay Bridge, construction of homes and warehouses, and railroad repair, while the women sold fabric materials and jewelry. Cunningham picked up a lifelong love of homemade jewelry from them. They played music in the evenings around the campfires. The family kept chickens and pigs and a goat in the back of their house. After Parole was annexed by the city in

1951, they could not replace any animals when they died, so once they were gone, there could be no new ones. Father Clem Wagner bought "stuff" at auctions and refurbished the goods into anything he could sell at the trading post. He loved fixing old guitars. When slot machines ended in Maryland, he bought many old ones, some of which still had coins in them. The police raided the post and destroyed the machines with sledge hammers. Undaunted, Wagner sold parts to the casinos in New Jersey and other places. He also refurbished guns and through a process of bluing the gun metal and refashioning the wood, made them like new again. When Cunningham's grandparents died, Clem and Sweetie Wagner took over.

The Route 2 of today did not exist at that time. It is now basically the dividing line between the city of Annapolis and Anne Arundel County. The roads through the area then were what is now Old Solomon's Island Road and West Street. Forest Drive was paved in the late 1950s, which split the property. The family leased the property where Office Depot is now to the Ethan Allen furniture company, which built a beautiful showroom and then years later moved to the new Annapolis Towne Center at Parole.

Lorna Cunningham grew up attending St. Mary's School downtown through 11th grade and then attended public school for her last year. Clem Wagner always looked after what he referred to as "the old folks" (he was in his late eighties himself) and would go to the churches and deliver their leftover bread to other older people. As it happened, both Clem and Sweetie Wagner got sick at the same time and were on different floors of the Anne Arundel Hospital. When Clem Wagner passed away, nurses rolled his wife into his room and said, "Sweetie, Clem has passed; he's stopped breathing." She looked at the door and said, "I'll never eat stale bread again!" By then it was the early 2000s. Until his last breath, Clem Wagner was giving the nurses crab cake recipes and teaching German to everyone who would listen. The Wagner property was bought and turned into a shopping center.

Source: Personal interviews by Joyce Edelson

Sports Teams in Parole

Finky's Termites basketball team of Parole, the Parole Giants baseball team, and the Parole Falcons were prominent sports teams in Parole. Parole and Bates High School had many excellent sports teams over the years. The basketball team sponsor was Finky's Grocery Store, which was located on West Street Extended.

Source: Janice Hayes-Williams

Finky's Termites Basketball Team

Doctors Faye Allen and Aris T. Allen and the Parole Health Center

Drs. Faye Allen (1921-2008) and Aris T. Allen (1910-1991), who met at Howard University Medical School in Washington, D.C., had a significant impact on the delivery of medical care to African-American residents of the Parole community. Until 1955, the Emergency Hospital (now Anne Arundel Medical Center) did not offer maternity care to pregnant black women in the community, and the alternatives were midwife delivery in their homes or long trips to black-owned hospitals in Washington D.C. or Baltimore. Dr. Aris T. Allen remembered putting at-risk laboring patients in his own car and driving them to Freedman's Hospital or Johns Hopkins Hospital. Due to the high infant mortality rate in Anne Arundel County, the health department eventually offered free prenatal and postpartum care to areas providing space to do so.

Parole Health Center at 1950 Drew Street
Image courtesy of Les Howard Studios

In 1936, under the guidance of Parole Elementary School Principal Walter S. Mills, Rev. John T. Chambers, Sr., and the PTA of the school, of which Chambers was president, the citizens of Parole secured the use of the Asbury Methodist Church in Parole (now Cecil Memorial United Methodist Church) for health services, especially prenatal and postpartum care. Drs. Faye and Aris T.

Allen could now examine patients behind sheets hung for privacy and provide appropriate care so babies were born healthy. Many of them were unable to pay for the care they needed at that time, but the Drs. Allen were determined to fulfill a need to the Parole community. After two years, the health center moved to Mount Olive Methodist Episcopal Church, which provided a sink and running water, but only a space heater in the winter months.

It soon became apparent that Parole, especially its African-American community, would need expanded health care. A fund-raising campaign began, and groundbreaking for a new facility at 1950 Drew Street took place in 1946 when land was purchased from Henry and Marie Taylor for $10. Some construction was contracted out, but most of the work was done by community residents. Dedicated in 1949, the health center's services included maternal and child health clinics and immunizations, including a Child Development Center, later the Head Start Center.

To meet the increasing needs of the community, a fund-raising campaign, headed by France Pindell, father of Alderwoman Rhonda Pindell Charles, began to raise funds to renovate and expand the health center. Through a combination of grants and donations from businesses and organizations, volunteers and coordinators, ground-breaking for the newly renovated health center began in 2001. Dedicated in 2002, the Parole Health Center is one of the most modern and well-equipped centers in Anne Arundel County. Services include Healthy Start home visiting and case management for pregnant women, infants, and toddlers, HIV/AIDS testing and counseling, immunizations, pregnancy testing, tuberculosis treatment, substance abuse treatment, and an expanded level of health services to the community. There is also a day care center, and a conference room.

The health center was recognized by the Annapolis City Council on December 19, 2016, as a city landmark, under the protection of the Historic Preservation Commission. It is the first such landmark outside the city's Historic District that still provides services to residents in need. The landmark designation does not change much for the health center itself. It still provides services to residents in need, but it does help protect the center if it were to become a target for demolition. Its landmark designation is more about its cultural significance than the building itself, so the property is not required to follow the strict renovation and repair guidelines like others within Annapolis' Historic District. Most importantly, the legacy of the founders has been fulfilled and maintained. The landmark cements that legacy.

This story of the Parole Health Center provides an excellent example of community commitment to improve the lives of all citizens.

Sources:
www.aahealth.org/centers-history-parole-health-center
Maryland Department of Health
Sue Glover, Rotarian and Health Care Provider

ARIS T. ALLEN MEMORIAL

In a triangle facing the section of Chinquapin Round Road (named after the chinquapin tree) that goes from West Street to Aris T. Allen Boulevard before becoming Forest Drive again stands the statue of Dr. Aris T. Allen, surrounded by the newly planted chinquapin trees and additional plants. Unlike many trees that drop their seeds which germinate and grow into new trees, the chinquapins spread through their root system. The nuts, similar to American chestnuts, had long been a source of food for Native Americans and animals. Due to construction of roads, sidewalks, utility lines, homes, and businesses, many root systems were killed and the trees were lost to the community.

Statue of Aris T. Allen
Image courtesy of Les Howard Studios

During the re-dedication of the park and celebration of the tree planting on April 28, 2018, members of the community recalled their early days of picking up the chinquapins that had fallen to the ground and roasting them in their homes. Alderwoman Rhonda Pindell Charles spoke about standing tall in preserving the past, promoting the present and protecting the future of the Parole community. Officers of the Greater Parole Community Association and members of the community spoke of their memories of what Parole was like in earlier days and what the chinquapin trees meant to them.

In partnership with Annapolis, the state of Maryland, and Greenpeace, the chinquapin trees are being restored to the community. The Greater Parole Community Association won an award for planting a total of 63 trees in the Parole community.

Text of the Aris T. Allen Memorial: "A man of honor…A Distinguished career of professional and public service…As a Medical Doctor…As a member of the Maryland State Legislature… As an appointee of The President of the United States, to serve his Country on the National level…And as a caring person who has served his community in so many other ways…To help people in need…To provide opportunity for every citizen…And to set an example that brings out the very best in us".

Thomas Somerville Company

The Thomas Somerville Company has as its slogan "155 years of service to the community." *Thomas Somerville Co. - Our First 150 Years* is a recently published book by Bill Beck on the history of the Somerville family company making and selling plumbing, heating, and air-conditioning supplies that began during the Civil War and still exists today. Their beautifully appointed store and warehouse in Parole is at the corner of Solomon's Island Road (Route 2) and Somerville Road. The bright green building and property runs for a block from Route 2 east to Old Solomon's Island Road. The founder, Thomas Somerville, was born in 1830 in Perth, Scotland. He, his wife Margaret, and their first two children came to America in 1855. Two more children were born here. Their arrival coincided with the many refugees of the Irish potato famine also arriving in America. They moved to Baltimore in 1858 and, with the beginning of the Civil War, moved two years later to Washington for a job at the Navy Yard. Somerville left the Navy Yard within a year and started his own small brass foundry. By 1863, the Washington Aqueduct began bringing Potomac River water into the city. This effort required plumbing for both drinking, which was not so pure at that time, and water for homes and businesses. There was also a need to remove the standing water from the city, so a terracotta tile business was started.

Somerville Store in Parole
Image courtesy of Les Howard Studios

By the time Somerville's three sons took over, they discontinued the brass foundry and transferred their work into more water and waste water treatment, which then encouraged residences and businesses to buy plumbing systems. Thomas Somerville, Jr., bought out his two brothers, James and William. In 1931, after suffering a fire, rebuilding, and then running out of space, they moved the business from 13th Street near the White House to their terracotta plant at 6th and Buchanan streets, N.E. While busy with other business and community services, one favorite past-time was watching the not so winning Washington Senators baseball team. The ditty of the day was "For most of the first half of the 20th century, Washington was first in war, first in peace, and last in the American League."

The third generation would soon take over: Thomas Somerville III and four siblings. Following the stock market crash in October of 1929, the economically debilitating Great Depression set in. Since much of Washington was employed by the federal government, the unemployment rate was not as high, which was good for the Somerville plumbing business because houses and businesses continued having water needs. The company was hit with union strikes, so things were not as smooth as they might have been for their bottom line. The company bought and sold many businesses around the Washington area over the years. The business had been expanding into other fields, such as building, during World War II. Somerville participated in building the temporary office buildings strewn all over the mall and anyplace else land could be found, as well as the Pentagon, all of which needed plumbing facilities. And there were more houses and businesses with similar plumbing needs, so business boomed during the war for Somerville. The company also bought storm window, kitchen cabinet and brick-making plants.

John Canney Harding, Jr., (fourth generation) served in the Pacific Theatre in World War II and in the Occupation of Japan that followed. He flew 20 feet off the ground over Hiroshima and once he got home, his hair fell out. He said nobody had told them about any effects of radiation from the super bomb. Once he arrived home, he took his place in the family business.

Annapolis was familiar to the family as one of them had graduated from the Naval Academy. The company purchased Southern Maryland Supply Company at Bladen and Calvert Streets. In 1955, the company leased the current Parole facility. Anna May Somerville (third generation) helped lay the cornerstone of the Annapolis branch in 1954. The late 1950s were difficult years for the company. They celebrated the centennial of the business in 1962 (one year late because there were so many business dealings going on). The Somerville property in Muirkirk between Beltsville and Laurel was sold to Borden. Once the computer age began in 1960, the company made a difficult decision to hire someone outside the family to get their own financial house in order. He stayed seven years, and the family considered that he had saved the company. Now two seats on the board of the company are reserved for family members. They remain successful, with a long and proud family heritage.

In 1923, the family purchased property in the community of Shady Side in Anne Arundel County, south of Annapolis. An old house was enlarged and a second one built. At first, some family members took the railroad to Annapolis, traveled to the Annapolis dock, and then boarded the *Emma Giles* for a boat ride south to Shady Side and the West River for a weekend of fun at "Somervilla." Building of the road between Washington and Annapolis and the prevalence of more automobiles provided an easier way to get to the property, an hour away. After Thomas, Jr., died, his widow, who lived nearly 23 years longer, became the de facto matriarch. "Boo Boo," as her grandchildren called her, left the property to her 16 grandchildren, but by that time it was sorely in need of maintenance and not used as much, so the family sold it in 1980. By 2010, the property needed further renovation or tearing down, so the new owners made the decision to tear down all the buildings—another piece of Anne Arundel County history living on only in pictures and memories.

Source: *Thomas Somerville Co. - Our First 150 years* by Bill Beck, reviewed by Joyce Edelson

Bowen's Farm Supply

Few Annapolis institutions have survived two generations, let alone involved three generations of one family serving the community. Bowen's Farm Supply is a highly successful example of this rare kind of business serving the public for many years in Parole on Riva Road. Orville and Dorothy Bowen opened their farm supply business in 1973, shortly after the Baldwin Service Center closed on Generals Highway and the Southern States franchise opportunity arose. They built the retail store in 1971 themselves, added the warehouse a couple of years later, and enlisted help from all seven of their children. Two of their offspring have stayed for all these years: Amy became Office Manager, Randy became Warehouse Manager, and son-in-law James Miller learned the trade from Orville and is now Store Manager.

Orville, who passed away in 2016, did everything a small, new businessman must do to earn the trust of the farming community

Bowen's Farm Supply
Image courtesy of Les Howard Studios

(he was himself a farmer and landscaper), and the business gradually grew by "doing the right thing by the customer." Dorothy, who cared about all people and was very religious, was the spiritual leader of the family and staff. Together, with their children and son-in-law, they worked six days a week at the store, building a business based on customer loyalty and word of mouth, not advertising. They serviced everything they sold, and if a customer had a problem with a product, they fixed it.

James Miller has been Store Manager for years, and all current staff have the same commitment to their evolving customer base, now more oriented to landscaping services and homeowners. This dedication to the customer is being passed to the next generation: first was James' daughter Jennifer (who moved on to be a Regional Representative with Stihl) and now son Joe, who has worked at the store "since he could walk."

Source: Bob Whitcomb, Rotarian, Sailor and Waterways Environmentalist

Light House Shelter and Light House Bistro

Light House, Inc., formerly the Lighthouse Shelter, has provided food, shelter, and support services for more than 25 years. Its mission is "to repair lives with compassion by providing shelter and services to prevent homelessness, and empower people as they transition toward employment, housing and self-sufficiency." Its new building at 10 Hudson Street, Annapolis (off West Street near Route 2) is welcoming and beautiful.

The former Lighthouse Shelter location at 202 West Street has been refurbished into the **Light House Bistro**. The space formerly housed the Levy Family grocery and drug store. The Bistro employs those who have been homeless and are trying to redirect their lives. The food is healthy and delicious, and the service is excellent. The Bistro project is about creating jobs. They have an advanced culinary training center, a Building Employment Success Training (B.E.S.T.) catering kitchen, and permanent supportive housing. Four apartments for former residents of the Light House are located on the second floor. The Bistro's mission is rebuilding lives in order to break the cycle of homelessness by providing living wage employment for those experiencing homelessness. They believe sustainable housing is not

Light House Shelter
Image courtesy of Les Howard Studios

Light House Bistro
Image courtesy of Les Howard Studios

possible without sustainable employment. This self-sustaining and revenue-generating enterprise supports workforce development and housing programs. The project also contributes to the revitalization and economic development of the West Street Corridor.

Looking for a place to have lunch or dinner or need to employ a caterer for a special occasion? Stop by or give a call: 410-424-0922. You will not regret it and you will be helping others who are less fortunate. Bon Appetit!

Sources: www.AnnapolisLightHouse.org; www.lighthousebistro.org; Discussions with staff by Joyce Edelson

Gardner Center

The Gardner Center on Forest Drive is a two-story brick retail and office complex of 26,000 square feet with parking spaces for 200 cars. Earnie and Margaret Gardner built the center in 1964, with the final section completed in 1986. A new brick facade and walkway were included. Family-owned businesses have been here for over 20 years, such as New to You, an inviting housewares and women's clothes thrift store, Savvas Barber Shop, Annapolis Opticians, The Drawing Board, and many others. Before the Aris T. Allen Boulevard expressway was opened in 1992, this part of Forest Drive from Riva Road through Parole to Chinquapin Round Road had been the main artery to the Annapolis Neck peninsula. Dr. Allen was instrumental in rerouting part of Forest Drive to a new expressway further south that bypassed the Parole neighborhood, instead of slicing through and displacing its residents. Sadly, he did not live to see its completion. The businesses on Forest Drive have survived and remain a vibrant part of the community. At an angle to the Gardner Center are two more strips of stores before Chinquapin Round Road, which serve as an entryway onto the continuation of Forest Drive and the Annapolis Neck. In addition, the Ron Gardner Center is located on Chinquapin Round Road.

Gardner Center
Image courtesy of
Les Howard Studios

Source: www.gardnercenter.com; Interviews with retail tenants by Joyce Edelson

Paul Bunyan Statue

Paul Bunyan, according to legend, could fell a forest with one swoop and used a hotcake griddle so large that men greased it by skating across it on slabs of bacon. All 20 feet of him stood as a landmark watching over Parole for 15 years atop Baldwin Service Center, a farm and garden supply company on General's Highway. People came from miles away to see the landmark statue.

Paul Bunyan Statue

In 2009, when the store went out of business, Mrs. Baldwin donated the statue to the Anne Arundel County Fairgrounds in Crownsville, just northwest of Annapolis. The Baldwin building was torn down and a new Toys R Us occupied the space. Before taking up his new position as the "welcomer-in-chief" to all the people and animals who visit the Fairgrounds, Paul Bunyan was repainted by the Busy Beavers 4-H Club. Now he holds a welcome sign to all who enter the Fairgrounds gate.

Source: www.aacountyfair.org

Parole Plaza Shopping Center

The Parole Plaza Shopping Center, which was located on the site of the current Annapolis Towne Center at Parole, lasted 40 years, from 1962 to 2002. The land had been owned by the Freedman family since 1958. Nearly 100 years had passed since Camp Parole, the Union Civil War prisoner-of-war exchange camp, had existed there. Some of the land that once housed Camp Parole turned into a then state-of-the-art shopping center for Annapolitans and nearby shoppers. It was accessible mostly via auto as the railroad lines to Annapolis had been gone for about 30 years. The Parole Plaza Shopping Center represented the latest adventure in retail and touted the slogan "better than you remember."

Parole Plaza Shopping Center

Unfortunately, the opening of a new shopping center was devastating to the downtown Annapolis stores. It seemed people wanted bigger and better shopping venues. There were 26 stores, including Woodward & Lothrop, Britt's Department Store (which included the Parole post office), Sears, Roebuck & Co., Read's Drug Store, Hickory Farms, Magruder's, Santa's Workshop, which opened between Thanksgiving and Christmas, and many more.

Once all the stores had been closed and the buildings abandoned, what could or should be built in its place? How could the county get rid of such a crumbling eyesore at the edge of the state's capital city? What avenue should the county take to make new buildings and development environmentally friendly and sustainable?

In the interim, downtown Annapolis had reinvented itself as a tourist destination built on its waterside and historic appeal. Small-scale shops and restaurants became the "in" thing and downtown Annapolis began to thrive again.

The 33 acres of the old Parole Plaza Shopping Center and additional acreage was designated a Parole Growth Management Area. The purpose was to focus on commercial opportunities, employment, and high-density residential development within a defined geographic area. That expanded area was bordered by Bestgate Road and Annapolis Commerce Park on the north, Solomon's Island Road (Route 2) to the west, the Gingerville community and the Parole area on the east, and Broad Creek near Harry S. Truman Parkway to the south. Located within that space would be the Anne Arundel Medical Park, Westfield Shopping Center (Annapolis Mall), Jennifer Square Shopping Center, Annapolis Plaza, Annapolis Restaurant Park, Forest Plaza, Festival at Riva, and Annapolis Harbour Center.

Memories abound of what existed before all the different commercial centers took over.   Forest Plaza, on Forest Drive between Riva Road and Solomon's Island Road, had once been home to the Colonial drive-in movie theater, then Hechinger's, and now Home Depot, and includes a side strip mall. The now-paved shopping center sloped downward toward the creek, making a perfect venue for a drive-in theater. Several residents of Parole spoke about hanging out on the periphery of the drive-in theater to watch the movies, all the while swatting mosquitos. Part of Forest Plaza had also housed the old Plaza Theatre at the corner of Forest Drive and Solomon's Island Road, which was taken over by Bertucci's and Outback Steakhouse.

Old Drive-in and Plaza Theater

The Festival at Riva Center at Riva Road and Forest Drive came more recently. Restaurants and businesses opened along both sides of Solomon's Island Road from West Street south to the new Aris T. Allen Boulevard and Forest Drive from Old Solomon's Island Road east to the Gardner Center, and Chinquapin Round Road was a mix of commercial and residential. Forest Drive had been the main route from Riva Road east until Aris T. Allen Boulevard was built.

The Parole Plaza Shopping Center property was sold to a developer, and demolition finally got underway in July 2005. In its place came the modern Annapolis Towne Center at Parole, consisting of mixed-use high-rise residential apartments, condominiums, restaurants, shops, and parking garages. The first tenants arrived October of 2008, and the official grand opening was held in May of 2009. The Parole Plaza Shopping Center became another distant memory.   There are five to six new developments in various states of construction between Route 50 and Admiral Cochrane Drive. The historical neighborhood surrounding Parole continues to change as it becomes surrounded by high-rise buildings. All the new development lies within Anne Arundel County, not the city of Annapolis.

Sources: www.aacounty.org/departments/planning; www.visitaac.com

Gresham House

This historic 2-1/2 story home in Edgewater, Anne Arundel County (south of Annapolis), was built by Attorney John Gresham II sometime after 1686 on land owned by land-grant pioneer Captain Edward Selby. Both the Gresham and the Selby families were influential in Maryland and Virginia during the colonial era.

Gresham House is most associated with Commodore Isaac Mayo (1794-1861) who received it from an uncle who had purchased it around 1765. Commodore Mayo fought in the War of 1812, the Second Seminole War (1835-1842), and the Mexican-American War (1846-1848). His career aboard U.S. ships is legendary, including his command of the U.S. African Squadron, beginning in 1852. Commodore Mayo, with his wife and daughter, occupied the property beginning in the early 19th century.

Gresham House
Image courtesy of Les Howard Studios

Commodore Mayo was instrumental in selecting the location for the United States Naval Academy and is buried on the Naval Academy grounds. Much of the area near the Edgewater property is named after him. Mayo died in 1861 at the age of 67.

Mayo also owned a plantation in Elkridge, south of Baltimore, in Howard County, and his wife inherited a plantation upon her father's death in what is now Columbia in Howard County. The Mayo family owned enslaved people who often ran away. The irony of going to Africa to further U.S. anti-slavery policy aboard the *USS Constitution* was not lost on Commodore Mayo.

Over the subsequent years, the property went through different owners and deteriorated badly. Parole Rotary Club Charter Member Leon Johnson and his wife Beverly, parents of nine children, purchased the property in 1984. The inside of the house had to be completely redone with installation of water, plumbing, electricity, insulation, heating, and air-conditioning. The wood had to be replaced in part and the foundation and walks were fortified and re-built. Gresham House was listed on the National Register of Historic Places in 1990.

The Johnsons had moved east in 1965. Leon Johnson ran Johnson Pools until his retirement at age 65. He received seven national design awards for the pools he created, one of which is at Gresham House with its very own grotto. The Johnsons also performed extensive work and renovation of the grounds around the property, including flush toilets near a huge gazebo where social events are held, windmill, lighthouse, pond, and other buildings either built or restored.

In the winter of their lives, the Johnsons sold the property to Anne Arundel County. This is a happy outcome for all and a continuing and beautiful memory due to the hard work and vision of a loving couple. The survival of Gresham House and the memories of its inhabitants represent the very best of living history. Thanks to the Johnsons for preserving a piece of local history.

Sources: National Register of Historic Places; Personal interviews of Beverly and Leon Johnson by Joyce Edelson

London Town

London Town—also called Londontown and Londontowne (the names were used interchangeably)—is a colonial town on the southern side of the South River that was created by legislation in 1683. Its location on a major north-south travel route helped it become a thriving town during the late 1600s and most of the 1700s. Travel, tobacco, and trade were the main reasons it existed. The town was also one of many local slave markets. London Town was also the Anne Arundel County seat until 1695 when Annapolis was designated both the county seat and colonial capital.

While the government move could have caused London Town to decline, for the first half of the 1700s, it actually helped. Moving the capital from St. Mary's City in southern Maryland, where the first stage of settlement occurred in the 1600s, to Annapolis meant

Londontown's Brown House
Image courtesy of Les Howard Studios

that more people would pass through London Town on their way to Annapolis. There was an increase in taverns, ferry keepers, and other businesses in London Town between 1700 and 1740. London Town was George Washington's last stop before taking the ferry across the South River and landing near Parole.

Once settlement and commercial patterns shifted both inland and northwards toward Baltimore, London Town did see a decline in its usage. Though it remained the biggest population center south of Annapolis for the rest of the 1700s, by 1800 there was really no town left. Most town lots had been consolidated into just a few owners. Alternative travel routes meant the town had no purpose as a crossroads and ferry destination.

In the 1820s, the brick tavern, originally constructed by William Brown in 1764, was turned into the County Almshouse. It and the surrounding 10 acres remained in use until the 1860s. The site opened to the public in 1972 as a public garden and house museum. Archaeological investigations in the 1990s and the creation of the private London Town Foundation in 1995 have allowed for more buildings to be reconstructed, and a new visitor center and exhibit hall has been on the site since 2005. Many events, including weddings and summer concerts, are held on the grounds. The buildings are large enough to house meetings and conferences, and there are many demonstrations of colonial gardening and living to enjoy.

Source: www.historiclondontown.org; Logan and Will Hottle, Rotarian family and volunteers at Historic London Town and Gardens

Public Gardens in the Area Open to the Public

Coretta Scott King Memorial Garden, at the former Sojourner-Douglass College Annapolis Campus, 135 Stepney's Lane, Edgewater

Hancock's Resolution Garden, 2795 Bayside Beach Road (one block from Bayside Beach), Pasadena

Helen Avalynne Tawes Garden, Department of Natural Resources, 580 Taylor Avenue (across from the Naval Academy Stadium), Annapolis

Herbarium at Anne Arundel Community College, 101 College Parkway, Arnold

Historic London Town & Gardens, 839 Londontown Road, Edgewater

William Paca House and Garden, 186 Prince George Street, Annapolis

ANNAPOLIS AND ANNE ARUNDEL COUNTY PUBLIC BOAT RAMPS

Annapolis has two public boat ramps at Truxton Park on Spa Creek in the Eastport area and also a boat ramp facility on Weems Creek which empties into the Severn River, known as the Tucker Street Boat facility, near the neighborhood of West Annapolis.

Anne Arundel County has a public boat ramp at Sandy Point State Park near the Chesapeake Bay Bridge. A new second boat ramp is at Smallwood State Park in Pasadena. Ahoy, Mates!

Carr's and Sparrow's Beaches (1926-1974)

In 1902, Frederick and Mary Wells Carr purchased 180 acres of farmland on the Annapolis Neck Peninsula with frontage on the Chesapeake Bay. Depending on which family member tells the story, Carr was either a runaway slave or a free black man. In either case, after 50 years of service to the United States Naval Academy, he was able to buy prime farm land. The land was farmed for around 20 years when Carr founded Carr's Beach. Florence Carr Sparrow, one of the daughters who inherited the family's land, created Sparrow's Beach in 1931, just north of Carr's Beach. The other daughter, Elizabeth Carr Smith, continued Carr's Beach. The other three children sold their shares of the estate to Florence and Elizabeth. The beaches and businesses operated side by side but were two separate entities. The two beaches attracted families and entertainment from around the country and were a vacation retreat for black families in the mid-Atlantic region. Many residents of Parole and Anne Arundel County frequented the beaches in the days of segregation and speak fondly of their memories. It was not unusual for a concert to attract crowds of over 10,000 fans. The last

Carr's Beach

concert hosted at the beaches was in 1973 with a performance by Frank Zappa.

During the summers black teachers worked at the beaches, teens parked cars, black bus companies handled transportation needs, and the state of Maryland profited from the slot machine and entertainment revenues. George Phelps, the first black sheriff in Anne Arundel County, hired 225 black men as special deputy sheriffs to keep law and order during the summer season. By the early 1960s when the civil rights movement ended the Jim Crow era, the popularity of Carr's and Sparrow's beaches diminished. Sandy Point State Park near the Chesapeake Bay Bridge was the newest attraction. Physically, the beaches no longer exist, but are still prominent in the happy memories of those who participated in the concerts and activities.

Charles Walker "Hoppy" Adams and WANN Radio Station
For 40 years, Annapolis 1190 AM WANN radio station disc jockey "Hoppy" Adams (1926- 2005), a resident of Parole, broadcast the concerts at Carr's Beach. According to John T. Chambers, Sr., who took "Hoppy" under his wing as a young man and taught him to cut hair, his nickname came from a bum leg due to polio. Adams quickly moved from barber shop to taxi cab, started his own cab company, and went on to broadcasting and WANN station manager and executive vice president. With 50,000 watts of power, WANN radio was able to broadcast beyond the Eastern Shore, north to Baltimore, and as far west as Ohio. Adams quickly attracted a large following and became the face of the station. Soon WANN became the "go-to" place for aspiring artists hoping the station would broadcast their latest singles. Businessmen vied for air time to advertise their products. Adams was a well-loved personality

and an ambassador for African-American culture. The plain tan wooden carrying box covered in wallpaper that Adams used for his broadcasts is now proudly displayed at the Smithsonian's National Museum of American History in Washington, D.C.

Through the Hoppy Adams Foundation in Annapolis, his legacy endures through their scholarship drive to fulfill his vision of ensuring positive atmospheres where students experience a sense of belonging, positive self-esteem, and awareness of the positive impact they can have in their communities.

WANN Radio Annapolis had been started by Morris Blum (1909-2005), a son of Jewish immigrants, born in Pennsylvania, who moved with his family to Baltimore in 1918. For a Boy Scout project, he built a crystal set receiver in their attic out of an oatmeal box. Fascinated with being able to receive voices through the air, Blum became a pioneer in broadcasting that may have started with that box. During World War II, Blum served in the Merchant Marines as a radio operator aboard a tanker and then worked in radio intelligence for the FCC. He founded WANN in 1946. After several years experimenting with "Back to Bebop" music, he moved toward broadcasting to an underserved African-American audience, hence the legendary heyday of the station. Subject to the whims of the market and the dominance of FM radio, the black music and news format was changed in 1992 to a growing country music audience, but with mixed results. Many locals were incredulous at the turn of events--move over, Michael Jackson, and make room for Garth Brooks! In 1999 the Blum family sold the station to WBIS, which switched to news-talk. Blum retired at the age of 88 and died at 95 in Annapolis. Now 1190 AM is the home of WRCW, of Washington, D.C., which presents Chinese business news in English. According to his sons, Jeffrey and Larry, their father used his radio station to champion human rights and racial equality. They also said what other people thought of him or his family really did not matter to him and that he fought bigotry his entire life. Also, he believed public service should not be ignored and forgotten and left his mark on a lot of broadcasters. The sons said he also had to endure a backlash from some in the Annapolis citizenry for serving the local African-American audience. Blum's sons said their father probably stayed with the station longer than he should have, but he felt he had employees and a community to serve. And so he did, respectfully and beautifully.

Sources:
Smithsonian magazine
www.blackpast.org
www.Carr'sBeach.com
www.Sparrow'sBeach.com

Kunta Kinte-Alex Haley (KKAH)
Monument and Foundation

In 1976, author Alex Haley (1921-1992) wrote *Roots: The Saga of an American Family*, based on researching the genealogy of his family back to an ancestor, Kunta Kinte, from The Gambia, Africa. He arrived in Annapolis in bondage in 1767. The story was made into a television series watched by millions.

Through the work of Leonard Blackshear (1943-2006), a past president of the Parole Rotary Club, and continued by his wife Patsy, the Annapolis City Dock contains the memorial to Kunta Kinte where he first arrived in Maryland in 1767. Alex Haley is portrayed reading to a group of children before him. Close by is the Leonard Blackshear Walk, with numerous plaques honoring his community work, reconciliation efforts, and founding of the Kunta Kinta-Alex Haley Festival held annually at City Dock. One of the plaques quotes a passage from *Roots*: "Millions of Africans were stolen from their families and forced to endure the horrors of the Middle Passage and slavery. The New World was built largely on their labor, on the subjugation of the Native Americans and on the indentured servitude of Europeans and Asians." Blackshear also founded the project Books for International Goodwill (BIG) while president of the Parole Rotary Club. He was a systems engineer and a successful businessman.

Leonard Blackshear Walk Plaque
Image courtesy of Les Howard Studios

Alex Haley Statue with children
Image courtesy of Les Howard Studios

Current KKAH Foundation activities include creating a documentary of former Bates High School teachers, as well as the Legacy Project, which encourages and assists people researching their heritage. The foundation's genealogy library is now housed on the second floor of the Asbury United Methodist Church on West Street in Annapolis, the oldest African-American church in Annapolis and Anne Arundel County. A genealogy specialist in residence is available one day a week to assist those interested in researching their roots.

Sources:
www.KinteHaley.org
Interview with Patsy Blackshear by Joyce Edelson

Pieces of Parole

The Point at Annapolis: It took much research and many years for Steve Muller to develop the former Johnson Lumber Company property of 1901 West Street at the corner of West Street and Chinquapin Round Road into a mixed-use complex of apartments and retail space. Historical markers in the inner courtyard behind the retail shops recite the history of the area.

Along West Street and Forest Drive, older houses and businesses were frequently torn down and new businesses were built in their place. That transformation continues to the present. The building that once housed a bowling alley at the corner of Chinquapin Round Road and George Avenue is now leased to Severn Auto Body and Regal Paint Store.

At the green-roofed Little Tavern which was located at 84 West Street, blacks had to order from the side window and wait outside, no matter the weather, for their orders to be put through the side window. Each burger cost 10 cents.

A roller skating rink in Annapolis was located on West Street, just west of Old Solomon's Island Road intersection. Another roller skating rink was located on George Avenue where Evolutions Gym is now located.

When a visiting carnival was put on an empty lot, blacks could attend only on the last two days. Blacks competed at the race track in Parole, but only against each other. The white track managers designated the third race of the day "for horses owned and driven by colored persons."

Source: *The Strange Career of Jim Crow* by C. Vann Woodward

Main restaurants welcoming blacks were Canton's on Taylor Avenue, Harley's sub shop, and English's chicken restaurant.

The library housed at the Reynolds Tavern was closed to blacks until 1940.

Pindell Field
Image courtesy of Les Howard Studios

Pindell Field in Bestgate Park on Bestgate is named after the Pindell family of Parole, which had many sport stars.

The Mount Olive Community Life Center at 4 Hicks Avenue, behind Mt. Olive AME Church, provides a meeting space for academic, social, and non-profit events.

Parole businesses included Hicks Upholstery and Tasker's Beauty Salon, both on Bunche Street. On Hicks Avenue, Miss Hamilton started a credit union for teachers so they could cash their paychecks.

Tasker Beauty Salon, 37 Bunche Street, was one of the few black-owned salons in Annapolis. Begun in 1957 by Alice Tasker Brown (nee Makell – 1920), it operated for nearly 50 years. The Browns had moved to Parole from South Anne Arundel County. After Brown passed away in 1989, her daughter, Beverly Downs, took over ownership and operation. Carla Downs is the third generation of this Parole family, currently living in the nearby house previously owned by her parents.

In 1946, George Phelps was appointed by Major Joe Alton as the first African-American deputy sheriff of Anne Arundel County, where he served for about 20 years. He began a security firm and later, with his wife Marion, opened a local chapter of Opportunities Industrialization Center, geared to training people for entry-level jobs. The Center continues in operation.

In 1994, Joseph Johnson was appointed by Mayor Alfred Hopkins as the first African-American Police Chief for the city of Annapolis, a post he held for 14 years before retiring.

Lou Hyatt and Michael Earle built many of the homes and apartment buildings in Parole beginning in the 1950s. Wood from the razed Camp Parole buildings had been used to build some early houses in Parole, as well as the Stanton School.

Source: Above Pieces of Parole are based on conversations between Editor Joyce Edelson and residents of Parole.

For More Information about Life in the Parole area:
Life in a Black Community – Striving for Equal Citizenship in Annapolis, Maryland, 1902-1952, by Hannah Jopling and published by Lexington Books, contains a wealth of historical information about Annapolis and Parole in the first half of the 20th century. We recommend her work to our readers. The book can be purchased through Amazon.

The Greater Parole Community Association (GPCA) and Tree Planting

The Greater Parole Community Association has been around since 1951. Principal Walter S. Mills and the Rev. John T. Chambers, Sr., began what was then the Parole Improvement Association. In the 1990s the name was changed to the Community Association of Parole, and in February 2014, the name changed again to its current name. So for 68 years, the community association has been advocating for everyone and everything that will preserve Parole as a viable, livable, lovable, and family-centered community.

On January 22, 2018, two board members of the Association, Lon Powell and Terence Wright, received citations from Annapolis City Mayor Gavin Buckley for their efforts in the Ward 3 Tree Planting Project. The City of Annapolis Office of Environmental Policy, Alderwoman Rhonda Pindell Charles, and GPCA partnered to offer citizens free trees to plant in their neighborhoods and on their property. Their goal was to plant 50 trees within the Parole (Annapolis) community. Not only did they meet their goal, they exceeded it, by having over 63 trees planted to enhance the aesthetics of Parole, as noted in the story of Aris T. Allen Memorial Park.

The tree planting opportunity afforded the GPCA an opportunity to reintroduce chinquapin trees to the local environment. Some of the trees are now surrounding the Aris T. Allen statue at the intersection of Aris T. Allen Boulevard and Chinquapin Round Road. These native trees were seen along Drew Street and Chinquapin Round Road several decades ago, but were lost during community development. Chinquapin trees have historical significance to the Parole community and are fondly remembered by senior members of the community who have reflected on the

Chinquapin Tree at the corner of Forest Drive and Chinquapin Round Road
Image courtesy of Les Howard Studios

days of old when the edible nuts from the trees were harvested, roasted, and eaten. The chinquapin is a sub-species of the chestnut family. It can grow up to 40 to 50 feet high and can spread 50 to 60 feet wide. Chinquapins are delicious eaten right out of the burr in the fall. Each burr has a single nut, unlike chestnuts that have nut divisions.

As Carla Downs, GPCA board member, noted: "Planting trees has many positive aspects. According to the Clean Air Gardening company, trees are like the lungs of the planet. They breathe in carbon dioxide and breathe out oxygen. Planting trees also reduces traffic noise, provides shade and cooling, increases real estate value, and decreases one's energy bill, along with other positive health and esthetic features. The entire community benefits when trees are added to the environment." Congratulations to the GPCA for their good work. GPCA's tree planting efforts were acknowledged in an article of the Annapolis Environmental Commission.

Source: Alderwoman Rhonda Pindell Charles and Carla Downs

How the Streets in Parole Got Their Names

What's in a name? Many streets in Parole have been named for distinguished people in the community.

Hoppy Adams Way was named after Charles Walker "Hoppy" Adams, a distinguished disk jockey, radio personality, and executive vice president with radio station WANN in Annapolis that served the largest black entertainment market in America outside of New York.

Parole / Drew Street Sign
Image courtesy of Les Howard Studios

Allen Drive was named for Dr. Aris T. Allen (1910-1991), an African-American physician, Maryland legislator, businessman, author, and humanitarian. He developed the Allen Apartments located on Allen Drive.

Bausam Drive was named for Fred Bausam, a white property owner in the Parole area who sold several lots to various African-Americans so they could purchase the land and build their homes in an area formerly known as John Neal's Farm. He lived during the early and mid-1900s.

Norwood Brown Lane was named after Thomas Norwood Brown, who was an entrepreneur, the first alderman of Parole, and an advocate for growth and development in the African-American community in Annapolis.

Bunche Street was named for African-American Dr. Ralph J. Bunche (1904-1971), a diplomat who won the Nobel Peace Prize in 1950 for his negotiation of the 1949 armistice between Israel and its Arab neighbors. He was an international civil servant and was awarded the Medal of Freedom by President Lyndon B. Johnson. Also named for him was the Ralph Bunche School located in southern Anne Arundel County, which served the African-American population prior to school desegregation.

Carver Street was named for African-American Dr. George Washington Carver (1864-1943), a scientist and agricultural chemist who earned his doctorate from the University of Rochester in 1941. He did extensive work at the Tuskegee Institute in Alabama and researched projects concerning Southern agriculture, especially peanuts and soybeans, that revolutionized the southern economy in the United States by liberating it from excessive dependence on cotton. Also named for him was the Carver Elementary School located in the Gambrills-West Anne Arundel County area, which served the African-American population prior to school desegregation. The Carver Center is still open for continuing education and special projects.

Center Street is located in the center between Forest Drive and Oaklawn Avenue and in the center between Forest Drive and Allen Drive, where the Allen Apartments are located. Decades ago, this area was heavily wooded. The true origin of the name Center Street is unknown.

Chinquapin Round Road has its name because, prior to homes and businesses being built there, the Chinquapin Round Road corridor consisted of many chinquapin trees.

Davis Street was named for the Davis family of Parole. Members of this African-American family were landowners and included brothers Charles, Ernest, and the Rev. William Henry Davis.

Dominoe Road has an interesting origin. During the residential development of the Parole community, it was "suggested" that African-American residents not be allowed to build their homes beyond a certain geographical area. Specifically, along the Forest Drive corridor, no African-American should build a home beyond the corner of Forest Drive and Dominoe Road going east, meaning the homes should be built only between Forest Drive and Old Solomons Island Road and Forest Drive and Dominoe Road, thus, creating a "dominoe [sic] effect" of home building. Several years later, certain persons attempted to stop the development of the African-American Forest Villa community, located east of Forest Drive and Dominoe Road. However, the attempts to stop the development of Forest Villa were defeated and, upon this defeat, the "domino effect" ceased to exist.

Dorsey Avenue was named for the Dorsey family of Parole, an African-American family that built most of the homes on this street. The family members consisted of several brothers and included Robert, William, and Joseph "Buck" Dorsey.

Dorsey Drive, located in the Dorsey Heights sub-community of Parole, was also named for the Dorsey family of Parole. This area was formerly known as Elias Wilson's Grove.

Drew Street was named for African-American Dr. Charles Drew (1904-1950), a scientist who was the first to develop the preserving technique for blood transfusions and the first to establish a blood bank, which started during the World War II era. Ironically, he died in a car accident after he could not receive the necessary blood transfusion that would have saved his life because of widespread discrimination during this time. The Community Health Center of Parole, Inc., appropriately, is located on Drew Street.

Forest Drive has its name because prior to homes being built in Parole, the Forest Drive area/corridor consisted of nothing but many trees. It was extremely wooded.

Gilmer Street was named for the Gilmer family of Parole. Members of this African-American family were landowners in this area and included former alderman Samuel Gilmer. This area also consisted of many chinquapin bushes.

Hicks Avenue was named for the Hicks family of Parole. Members of this African-American family were landowners who had purchased this property from the Hausclaw family. Some members of this family include James, "Jumbo," Harvey, Joe, Dorothy, and Ruth Hicks Chambers.

Holeclaw Street was named for Lewis Hausclaw (the correct spelling), an African-American landowner in the Parole area who sold lots to African-Americans so they could build homes, and his family. He lived during the late 1800s and early 1900s.

Kirby Lane was named for the Kirby family of Parole that include Ellen and Richard Kirby, Delores Brown Luck, and J. William and J. Irving Swann

Lee Street was named for the Lee family of Parole, including Randolph Lee (who was killed during World War II), Temperance Simms, and Emory Lee.

Lincoln Drive may have been named for the 16th President of the United States, Abraham Lincoln (1809-1865). In 1862, President Lincoln authorized the signing of the Emancipation Proclamation, which meant that, as of January 1, 1863, all slaves in rebellion would be free. However, the true origin of the name Lincoln Drive is unknown.

Link Street is located between the "links" Forest Drive and Oaklawn Avenue. Decades ago, this area was heavily wooded. However, the true origin of the name Link Street is unknown.

Louis Drive may have been named for African-American, Joe Louis (1914-1981), born Joseph Barrow, who became the World Heavyweight Boxing Champion in 1937. However, the true origin of the name Louis Drive is unknown.

Middle Street is located between or in the "middle" of Drew Street and Vincent Street. The true origin of the name Middle Street is unknown. Since this list was originally published, Middle Street has been renamed **George and Marian Phelps Lane**. George Phelps was the first African-American Deputy Sheriff in Anne Arundel County. He also owned a security firm, and he and his wife opened a local chapter of Opportunities Industrialization Center to train people for entry-level jobs, specializing in helping former prisoners. He was the uncle of Annapolis Historian Janice Hayes-Williams.

Neal Street was named for the Neal family of Parole, who were African-American landowners. This area was formerly known as Dan Neal's Grove.

Oaklawn Avenue has its name because prior to homes being built in Parole, this area consisted of many oak trees. It was extremely wooded.

Old Solomon's Island Road was named for the area "Solomon's Island," located in southern Maryland. The Old Solomon's Island Road area was formerly known as South River Road and Beaver Dam Hill.

Parole Street was named for the community in which it is located. Most of the homes in this area were built by William and Smalley Dorsey.

Reidsville Street was named for the Reid family of Parole, who were African-American landowners. A family cemetery is located to the rear of Reidsville Street.

Rosewood Street may have been named for the beautiful roses that had been planted there. Decades ago, this area was heavily wooded. However, the true origin of the name Rosewood Street is unknown.

Robert Small Road was named for African-American serviceman and statesman Robert Smalls (1839-1915), who was born into slavery in South Carolina. His expertise as a pilot on boats during the Civil War was so phenomenal that it gave him a chance to win his freedom. He later served as a South Carolina state legislator for seven years and in the United States House of Representatives for nine years. It is appropriate that a street in the Parole community—a community established during the Civil War—would be named for a Civil War hero.

Noah Taylor Way was named after Noah Taylor, the foundation of a long-standing family of community supporters, who purchased one of the largest tracts of land in the Parole community. Nearly a century later, his descendants still own and occupy the land.

Vincent Street was named for the son of the first property owner on Vincent Street, Harrison Price, an African-American whose son's name was Vincent Price (1948-1981). Some members of Vincent Price's family include Alice Boston Collison and her daughter Enid Collison-Lee, who both resided, along with their families, on Vincent Street.

West Street (and West Street Extended) runs in an east-west direction. This area was formerly known as Camp Parole Road.

Source: Compiled by Lillian (Chambers) Burgess, Esther (Herndon) Blackstone and Alderman Samuel Gilmer for inclusion in the program celebrating the 1995 re-opening of the Parole Elementary School as the Walter S. Mills-Parole Elementary School, entitled "Celebrating 130 Years of Spirit – Parole Week" and reproduced here with permission of City of Annapolis Ward 3 Alderwoman Rhonda Pindell Charles. There have been additional streets in Parole added to this list, named for distinguished people of Parole.

Chambers Park, located on Dorsey Avenue, was named for the Chambers family of Parole who donated the property for the park.

Chambers Park
Image courtesy of Les Howard Studios

Some members of this family include John Wesley Chambers; his daughters Lillian Burgess, Susie Chambers, Katrina Wright, and Marie Stepney; his son John T. "Sonny" Chambers, Sr.; and his grandson and former City of Annapolis Mayor John T. Chambers, Jr.

For More Information about the History of Parole
Several years ago the Greater Parole Community Association sponsored a flyer entitled "Walk Parole – A Scavenger Hunt for History." Great care and effort went into the preparation, historical accuracy, and significance of all 20 points of interest described in the flyer. We recommend the flyer to our readers for further education and understanding of the historical significance of the area known as Parole. The flyer is available online.

Part II: Historical Background

Dodon Plantation (now Dodon Farm)

As with many family and land histories, differing versions exist. The story of the 550-acre Dodon Farm and the family of George Steuart, who came to America from Perthshire, Scotland, circa 1721, is no exception. Even the origination of the name "Dodon" has several explanations. However, enough of the record exists, including a partial family tree, to offer a brief overview.

The farm is located about 10 miles southwest of Annapolis near the South and Patuxent Rivers on Dodon Road, in Davidsonville, Maryland. The property was owned by Stephen Warman and sold in 1747 to Dr. George H. Steuart, a physician, tobacco planter, horse breeder, and politician. Beef cattle and thoroughbred horses were raised on the farm and tobacco was grown using slave labor, penal labor, and indentured servants.

The Steuart family grew wealthy in colonial times, and their influential political participation in the early days of Maryland is documented. George Steuart served as Mayor of Annapolis from 1759 to 1763. However, their prosperity was reduced by the American Revolution when Steuart had to make a decision to remain loyal to Scotland and the property his family retained there or join the American rebels. He chose to return to Scotland to inherit the family estate in Perthshire, but his family stayed in this country and he never again saw his family.

During the War of 1812, Steuart's descendants and other family members led Maryland volunteers, known as the Washington Blues, at the Battle of Bladensburg and the Battle of North Point and also fought in the Battle of Baltimore. Their large family's political influence and medical heritage continued through the generations.

During the Civil War, the slave-holding Steuarts supported the Confederacy, with many of them fighting for the south. The result of their choice was that much of the family property in several locations throughout Maryland was seized by the federal government.

Dodon Farm survived. Since 1743, eight generations of the Steuart family have continued working the family farm. The mansion burned down around 1790, was replaced with another around 1800 which also burned down in 1953, leaving only the ruins. The family cemetery on the farm carries a great deal of its family members' history. An additional cemetery that belonged to the Catholic Church when it owned the farm (between 1890 and 1929) also remains on the farm. Annette Steuart Pittman bought the farm back from the church, restoring it to the family. She was the great-grandmother of Steuart Pittman, Jr., who, along with several siblings, currently runs the farm. The property now includes farming, an equestrian center, a horse-breeding operation, and a vineyard.

The land has been preserved through the Maryland Agricultural Land Preservation Foundation. This preservation status will ensure that no further development of the land will be permitted.

Sources: Maryland Archives; Dodon Farm websites

Patuxent River

A little-remembered fact about the 115-mile long Patuxent River emptying into the Chesapeake Bay is that ocean-going vessels once plied its waters. The part of the river closest to Parole is about 10 miles west and runs under the Route 50 bridge. The Patuxent is the largest and longest river entirely within Maryland; the river and its watershed lies entirely within the state.

During the War of 1812, the British entered the Chesapeake Bay and headed up the Patuxent River to get to Washington, D.C. The American Navy had a small flotilla of gunboats on the Patuxent. The narrow Patuxent River enabled the smaller American ships to move easily, but slowed the ocean-going British ships. The two fleets engaged in skirmishes, both aboard ships and on surrounding land. However, the Americans were no match and chose to burn and scuttle their own ships to prevent them from falling into the hands of the enemy. The British, traveling overland, then defeated a U.S. force at Bladensburg in Prince George's County on August 14, 1814. That same day British forces entered Washington, D.C., and set fire to government buildings, including the U.S. Capitol and the White House. The wrecks of the ships scuttled in the Patuxent River have been located near present-day Lothian and are being excavated.

Silting and erosion over many years and pollution from development in its upper smaller rivers has rendered the Patuxent River impassible for large ships. Had the Patuxent been dredged, Upper Marlboro in Prince George's County might have been the busiest seaport in Maryland as it is nearer the Atlantic Ocean than is Baltimore.

But it was the 39-mile-long Patapsco River further north emptying into the Chesapeake Bay that was dredged to accommodate the larger ships, making Baltimore the busiest seaport in Maryland. Access to Baltimore's port also accommodated goods and produce from the entire East and Midwest. The Baltimore port continues to thrive to this day. In the meantime, the Patuxent just keeps rolling along, providing recreational and boating activities for many, thanks to preservation efforts and wetlands sanctuaries.

Sources: www.Maryland.gov; Colonial maps; Annapolis Convention Digital Encyclopedia; www.History.com; *Maryland Gazette*; Articles in *Bay Journal* and *Bay Weekly*

Maryland Nicknames

The Old Line State

This name came from the 400 regular line troops from Maryland who fought, along with troops from other colonies, against 15,000 of the 50,000 British soldiers and Hessian mercenaries. A huge armada of 400 British warships had sailed into New York Harbor in the summer of 1776 during the Revolutionary War. The British objective was to stamp out the American rebels in what became known as the Battle of Brooklyn. It was during this battle that 21-year old Nathan Hale, a teacher, soldier, and spy for George Washington, was hanged for treason with his memorable line, "I regret that I have but one life to give for my country." The Marylanders drew together under their Baltimore-born commander, Major Mordecai Gist. Against overwhelming odds of 10 to 1, the Marylanders charged the British troops again and again, holding the line against the British. In viewing the encounter through a spyglass, Washington reportedly said, "Good God, what brave fellows I must this day lose!" The Maryland 400 held the line and engaged the British forces long enough for George Washington and the rest of his Continental Army and equipment to escape across the East River. A storm had rolled in, and both sides waited it out. Under dense fog and much to the surprise of the British, Washington, his equipment, and most of his army were able to join the rest of the Continental army in Manhattan. The Continental army would fight another day. The courageous stand of the Maryland 400 gave rise to the "old line" nickname. Maryland lost 256 of the 400 men in that battle. Noted artist Alonzo Chappel captured the battle in a mid-19th century painting, available to see on line, along with a detailed description of the battle and the Continental Army's escape. A plaque dedicated to the Maryland

400 is displayed at the American Legion Post in the Gowanus neighborhood of Brooklyn.

Sidebars: Scholars at the Maryland State Archives and the Maryland Society of the Sons of the American Revolution have worked together on "Finding the Maryland 400." They have been able to document the lives of many Marylanders who fought in the early stages of our country. The 19th century historian Thomas Field called the stand of the Maryland Line "an hour more precious to American liberty than any other." The regiment roster and biographies of the soldiers can be found on line at msamaryland400.wordpress.com/.

Numerous organizations are involved in a "dig" near the American Legion Post in an effort to locate the remains of the soldiers who gave their lives for our fledging country in the Battle of Brooklyn.

The Free State

This name was based on Maryland being considered the birthplace of religious freedom in America when formed by George Calvert in the early 17th century as an intended refuge for persecuted Catholics from England. Catholics could live and worship here, but they could not vote at that time.

An additional explanation for the Free State nickname is based on the new Maryland Constitution, which took effect on November 1, 1864, providing that slavery within the State's borders was abolished. Maryland did, indeed, become a free state. The Emancipation Proclamation freeing all slaves in states in rebellion against the federal government had been signed by President Abraham Lincoln on January 1, 1863. Because Maryland had never seceded from the union and therefore was not formally in rebellion, it was left to the state of Maryland to free all slaves within its borders, which it did with its new Constitution, 1 year and 10 months later.

Sources: www.Maryland.gov; www.statesymbol.org

Maryland State Flag

Maryland's flag is shown on the back cover of this book. The black and gold (or yellow) chevron design of alternating colors on the flag represents the Calvert paternal coat of arms, beginning with George Calvert, 1st Baron Baltimore (1580-1632). George Calvert died five weeks before the new charter for Maryland from England's Charles I was sealed, leaving the settlement of the Maryland colony to his son Cecil, 2nd Baron Baltimore.

The red and white design with the bottony cross—a symbol of Christianity—comes from the coat of arms of George Calvert's maternal family, the Crosslands. Since George Calvert's mother was an heiress, he was entitled to use both coats of arms in his banner. Maryland's flag is the only U.S. state flag directly based on English heraldry. The Maryland flag is also the only state flag to have a Cross at the top of the flag pole. Both the Calvert and Crossland coats of arms were carried in the Crusades.

The symbols in the Maryland flag became conflicted during the Civil War, with the state of Maryland divided. The soldiers from Maryland who served in Robert E. Lee's Army of Northern Virginia and sympathized with the South often wore red and white cross bottony pins on their Confederate uniforms. The black and gold colors were used in the flags and uniform pins of the Marylanders who sided with the Union and served in the northern Army of the Potomac. Once the war was over, and the slow process of reconciliation began, the flag of both the Calvert and Crossland colors began appearing at public events in Maryland. The current flag was first flown in 1880 in a Baltimore parade marking the 150th anniversary of the founding of Baltimore. In 1888, it was flown at the Gettysburg Battlefield in Pennsylvania during ceremonies dedicating monuments to the Maryland Regiments. However, it wasn't until 1904 that the design on the front cover with both the Calvert and Crossland colors was declared the official state flag by the Maryland General Assembly.

In a recent story of the history of Maryland's Flag appearing in *Baltimore* magazine, Senior Editor Ron Cassie wondered if Marylanders should fly any flag paying homage to the Calvert family, either black and gold or red and white. Cassie listed some of the history of the Calverts and their proprietorship of Maryland. He reported that in 1639, at the direction of Cecil Calvert, 2nd Baron Baltimore, Maryland became the first colony to specify that baptism as a Christian did not make a slave a free person, as it did in England. In 1664, Charles Calvert, 3rd Baron Baltimore, and a plantation owner, directed that Maryland would be the first colony to mandate lifelong servitude for all black slaves, the first to make children of slaves their master's property for life, and the first to ban interracial marriages.

Despite the mixed history of the flag and slavery in Maryland, the Maryland state flag remains popular and is one of the most colorful and distinctive state flags.

Sources: www.50states.com; www.maryland.gov; www.baltimoremagazine.com

Maryland State Song: "Maryland, My Maryland"

The melody of the state song, "Maryland, My Maryland," incorporates "O Tanenbaum," a German folk song, and "O, Christmas Tree," an English folk song translated from the original Deutsche (German).

A Tannenbaum is a fir tree and the song refers to the fir's evergreen quality as a symbol of constancy and faithfulness. The Tannenbaum fir tree was not initially associated with Christmas.

The song actually originated in Silesia, formerly an Eastern German province now located chiefly in Poland. Melchior Franck (1580-1639) was born in Zittau (Saxony), Germany and died in Coburg (Bavaria), Germany. He was the composer who wrote the original music and lyrics for "Ach Tannenbaum" in 1615, based on the Silesian folk song. Franck is credited with bringing the Venetian School of Music north across the Alps into Germany, according to the *New Grove Dictionary of Music and Musicians*.

Ernst Anschutz (1780-1861), who was born in Suhl and died in Leipzig in the German state of Saxony, was a teacher, organist, poet, and composer who wrote the lyrics to "O Tannenbaum," based on Franck's German folk song. Anschutz' version penned in 1824 is the best-known version. The lyrics have been re-written many times over the centuries, and the song is played for many organizations and events.

The song and new lyrics came to Maryland via James Ryder Randall (1839-1908). His father, James A. Ryder, S.J., was the 20th president of Georgetown University. James Ryder Randall was born in Baltimore and taught school in Louisiana during the early part of the Civil War. It was during his time in Louisiana and a subsequent move to Georgia that he penned "Maryland, My Maryland." Unable to serve in the Confederate Army due to tuberculosis, Randall did serve with the Confederate States Navy in Wilmington, North Carolina. After the war, he became a newspaper editor and a correspondent in Washington, D.C., for *The Augusta Chronicle*.

The Pratt Street riots in Baltimore provided the impetus for James Ryder Randall to pen the words that would later become the state song. The riots took place in 1861, five days after the surrender of Fort Sumter in South Carolina. The 6th Massachusetts Infantry was changing trains en route to fight the South when an unruly mob of Southern sympathizers blocked the train tracks with timbers and anchors. The soldiers were ordered to fire into the mob until the police arrived. Casualties included eight rioters, one bystander, and three soldiers. Police Marshal Proctor Kane, appointed by newly elected Mayor George William Brown, put his policemen between the two groups and escorted the troops to Camden Station, where they boarded the train and left Baltimore. Thus the 6th was the first unit in the Union army to suffer casualties in the Civil War. Numerous paintings of the riots are online. To prevent further riots and protect the city of Baltimore as well as Fort McHenry, Baltimore was placed under military law. Randall has been referred to as the "Poet Laureate of the Lost Cause."

In "Maryland, My Maryland," Randall's lyrics refer to the Unionists as Northern scum and to President Abraham Lincoln as a tyrant. Randall called Marylanders cowards for failing to join Virginia in secession from the Union.

Of the nine verses of Randall's poem, only the third stanza is performed by the Naval Academy Glee Club because it has no Confederate battle cry lyrics. The University of Maryland Marching Band suspended the playing of the state song at its home football games. The decision was made after the deadly white supremacist rally took place in Charlottesville, Virginia, in August of 2017. The University of Maryland School of Music has launched a competition that invites University of Maryland students to write lyrics for a new state song.

The Maryland General Assembly had adopted Randall's version as our state song in 1939, the same year the movie *Gone with the Wind*, which romanticized the Old South, debuted. Many individuals, legislators, and organizations have repeatedly attempted to have "Maryland, My Maryland" removed as the state song because of its racist and secessionist lyrics. New versions to replace the current song have been presented to the General Assembly. The effort to have a new state song (lyrics and melody) presented and approved by the General Assembly continues by groups and individuals, including the editor of this book, Joyce Edelson, who welcomes all ideas. Contact her via e-mail at JoyceEdelson@gmail.com.

Sources: www.maryland.gov; www.historynet.com/baltimore-riot-of-1861.htm

The National Anthem: "The Star-Spangled Banner"

The Maryland state song is not the only controversial song written by a Marylander during the early part of our nation's history. The national anthem of the United States was not without its detractors. Francis Scott Key (1779-1843) who often wrote poetry and hymns, was born in then Frederick County (now Carroll County) and was a graduate of St. John's College in Annapolis, with an auditorium there named after him. He read law under an uncle and represented both slaves and slave owners in his career. He was nominated for U.S. Attorney by 7th President Andrew Jackson, a post in which he served from 1833 to 1841, using his position to suppress abolitionists—those who worked to end the practice of slavery. The abolitionists ridiculed his words and proposed that America was more like the "land of the free and home of the oppressed." Key was a founding member and active leader of the American Colonization Society, whose primary goal was to send free African-Americans back to Africa. He was once quoted as referring to blacks as "a distinct and inferior race of people." Key resigned from the Society's board in 1833 as its policies shifted toward abolitionism. However, Key publicly criticized the cruelty of slavery and volunteered to represent blacks, both free and enslaved. Once a slave owner, Key freed his slaves in the 1830s. Key is recognized more for changing his views on the moral wrongs of slavery than his earlier days as a slave owner.

His most famous legal case was the prosecution of Richard Lawrence for his unsuccessful attempt in 1835 to assassinate President Andrew Jackson at the entrance doors and top steps of the unfinished U. S. Capitol, the first attempt on the life of an American President. Lawrence was found not guilty by reason of insanity and spent the remainder of his life in asylums. Key argued numerous cases before the U.S. Supreme Court.

Key is best remembered for writing the poem that would become America's national anthem a hundred years later, "The Star-Spangled Banner." He was on a ship traveling to Baltimore during the War of 1812 when the Battle of Baltimore-Fort McHenry took place (September 12-15, 1814). His ship and others were prevented from continuing due to the battle between the American and English ships that fought for control of Baltimore Harbor. Fort McHenry was named after James McHenry (1753-1816), an American statesman, a Scots-Irish immigrant, a surgeon-soldier, a delegate to the Continental Congress from Maryland, a signer of the United States Constitution, and the third Secretary of War. The fort was built in 1799 on a small island in Baltimore Harbor to protect Baltimore during the Quasi-War with France (1798-1801). Sea battles between the new American Navy and French mercenary privateers who were seizing and plundering American merchant ships took place off the Barbary Coast of Northern Africa as well as the Caribbean and home waters. Hostilities ceased on September 30, 1800, partly because France was occupied with wars in Europe involving Great Britain, which ultimately led to the War of 1812 in America. The poem Key wrote after seeing the U.S. flag being hoisted over Fort McHenry would later become the national anthem. Key inserted some controversial lines into the third stanza decrying the former slaves who were then working for the British army against the United States. Key's poem about the Battle of Baltimore-Fort McHenry was recognized for official use by the United States Navy in 1889 and by 28th President Woodrow Wilson in 1916. It was made the national anthem by a congressional resolution on March 3, 1931, and signed by 31st

President Herbert Hoover.

"The Star-Spangled Banner," the country's most patriotic song, is sung or played before many sports games. Key's law office on Court Street in Frederick, Maryland, still stands. His memory is preserved on historical plaques, schools, college halls, bridges, parks, and a U.S. Navy submarine named after him. His writing of hymns and other songs merited his induction into the Songwriters Hall of Fame in 1970.

The melody for the national anthem came from the tribute to a Greek lyric poet named Anacreon who wrote in the ancient Ionic dialect. The lyrics to the original song, "To Anacreon in Heaven," were written around 1776 by the Anacreontic Society president and British lyricist, Ralph Tomlinson (1744-1778). The melody was composed by John Stafford Smith (1750-1836), a British composer, organist, and early musicologist. The song became the official song of the Anacreontic Society, an 18th-century gentlemen's club of amateur musicians in London. The melody to this popular English drinking song heard so often in this country started with the memory of a Greek poet in England and then traveled to America.

Sources: www.Maryland.gov; *Baltimore* magazine, March 2018; *Smithsonian* magazine, retrieved August 13, 2018; *Washington Examiner*, retrieved August 9, 2018; *The New Grove Dictionary of Music and Musicians*; www.umd.edu

NAMESAKES

The neighborhood of Parole in the state of Maryland has been a part of both Anne Arundel County and the City of Annapolis. We know how Parole got its name, but from where did the state, the county, and the city derive their names?

State of Maryland

The state of Maryland is named after England's Queen Mary (1609-1669), born Henrietta Maria, daughter of King Henry IV of France and Marie de Medici of Italy, who became the wife of Charles I, King of England, Scotland, and Ireland (1600-1649) of the Royal House of Stuart. Mary is an Anglicization of Henrietta Maria.

Queen Mary

In 1632 Charles I granted the charter for Maryland to George Calvert, the first Baron Baltimore. Charles I named the colony Maryland after his wife, Henrietta Maria (Queen Mary). On March 25, 1634, the first settlers arrived aboard two ships, the *Ark* and the *Dove*, in what would become Maryland's first capital, St. Mary's City. The site of the first capital is located on the western shore of the Chesapeake Bay in southern Maryland, just north of where the Potomac River empties into the Chesapeake Bay. Maryland Day is celebrated on March 25th every year.

Queen Mary gave birth to two future kings of England, Charles II and James II. Three of her grandchildren, William III, Mary II, and Anne, also reigned. Mary and Charles had nine or ten children, most of whom did not live to adulthood. Queen Mary, for whom Maryland is named and wife of Charles I, was the paternal grandmother of William III and his first cousin (also his wife), Mary II, and her sister Anne, for whom Annapolis is named.

Queen Mary lived another 20 years after her husband was executed for treason during England's first Civil War. After 11 years under Lord Oliver Cromwell and his son Richard, the monarchy was restored to Charles II, first son of Queen Mary and Charles I. Queen Mary died during the reign of her first son. (See the Royal House of Stuart succession below.)

It was England's Royal House of Stuart that oversaw the early settlers of Maryland. The colony was financed by Anne Arundel and Cecil Calvert, second Baron Baltimore, as noted below in the section on Anne Arundel County. Maryland would not have become the state it is, were it not for the early support of the Calverts, the Arundels, and the seven Stuart monarchs of England.

Source: *Maryland State Archives*

Sixteen Counties in Maryland with English Roots and Namesakes

Anne Arundel: Anne Arundel (or Arundell) Calvert, the wife of Cecil Calvert, second Baron Baltimore and first proprietary governor of the province of Maryland

Baltimore: Cecil Calvert, second Baron Baltimore, and the town of Baltimore in County Longford, a title in the Peerage of Ireland

Calvert: Calvert, family name of the Barons of Baltimore

Caroline: Lady Caroline Eden, wife of Maryland's last Colonial Governor, Robert Eden

Carroll: Charles Carroll of Carrollton, also known as Charles Carroll III, signer of the Declaration of Independence

Cecil: Cecil Calvert, second Baron Baltimore, first proprietary governor of the province of Maryland

Charles: Charles Calvert, third Baron Baltimore

Dorchester: Earl of Dorset (a county in southwest England), family friend of the Calverts

Frederick: Frederick Calvert, sixth Baron Baltimore (Frederick was briefly the capital of Maryland during the Civil War)

Harford: Henry Harford, illegitimate son of Frederick Calvert, sixth Baron Baltimore

Kent: Kent, a county in southeastern England

Prince George's: Prince George of Denmark, consort to Queen Anne

Queen Anne's: Queen Anne of Great Britain who reigned when the county was established in 1706

Somerset: Mary, Lady Somerset, daughter of Thomas Arundell of Wardour and sister of Anne Arundell Calvert, for whom Anne Arundel County is named

Talbot: Lady Grace Talbot, wife of Sir Robert Talbot, an Anglo-Irish statesman and sister of Cecil Calvert

Worcester: Mary Arundell, daughter of Sir John Arundell, sister to Lord Thomas Arundell, and the wife of Sir John Somerset, who was a son of Henry Somerset, first Marquess of Worcester, West Midlands, Worcestershire, England

Source: Maryland State Archives

Anne Arundel County

Anne Arundel County was named after the English noblewoman Anne Arundel Calvert (1615-1649), sometimes spelled Arundell or Arrundell. She was the daughter of Lord Thomas Arundell, first Baron Arundell of Wardour, an area located about 90 miles south of London in West Sussex, at the port of Arundell

Anne Arundel

on the Arun River and where Arundell Castle is located. Lord Arundell received his title for his fight against the Ottoman Turks in Hungary. However, his receiving a foreign title displeased Queen Elizabeth I, which led to a long history of conflict with the royals. The story of Lord Arundell could occupy more than a few seasons on British television, given his colorful life.

Anne or Ann was the product of Lord Arundell's second marriage to Anne Philipson. At the age of 13, Anne Arundel married Cecil Calvert, then 18, second Baron Baltimore. Both sets of parents supported their establishment of the new English colony of Maryland in America. Anne and Cecil oversaw their nine children, only three of whom survived to adulthood, and the new Maryland colony from Hook Farm Manor, built near Arundell Castle. A son of Cecil and Anne was Charles Calvert, third Baton Baltimore. After Lord Arundell's death, the couple funded the new colony with her inheritance, although neither ever visited the colony they helped found. After Anne's death at the age of 34, the Maryland General Assembly voted to name Anne Arundel County in her honor. A neighborhood named Wardour is located in Annapolis near the Naval Academy.

The website for Arundel Castle includes beautiful pictures and a history of the nearly 1,000 years of its existence. Arundel Castle has been featured in several movies and has doubled for Windsor Castle in other movies. The English kings, lords, dukes, and earls involved in the history of the castle's building, destruction, restoration, and preservation could easily occupy a decade of British television.

Note from Joyce Edelson: I toured England's Arundel Castle in the 1980s, an experience I will long remember. Family members continue to live in one of its wings. Much of the rest is open to the public. I had no idea at that time I would later move to Anne Arundel County, Maryland. In England, the castle's name is pronounced "Aarondale," with an emphasis on the first syllable, so it took me awhile to get used to pronouncing Arundel the Maryland way.

Sources: www.Maryland.gov; www.ArundelCastle.org

City of Annapolis

The name of the City of Annapolis is derived from "Anne" for then Princess Anne and "polis," which means an ancient Greek city/state. Annapolis was named after England's then Princess Anne (1665-1714) by Sir Frances Nicholson, Royal Governor of Maryland, when he moved the capital from St. Mary's City to Annapolis and needed a name for the new capital. Anne was the second daughter of James II and his first wife, Anne Hyde, Duchess of York.

Princess / Queen Anne

Princess Anne succeeded to the throne after the death of William III, known as William of Orange (the Netherlands), son of another Mary who was the sister of Charles II and James II. William III was therefore a nephew of both Charles II and James II. William III married then Princess Anne's older sister (also named Mary who became Queen Mary II), his first cousin. William and Mary reigned jointly from 1689 to 1702. Mary II died in 1694, after which William III ruled alone. There was one stillborn child, leaving Anne next in line to the throne.

None of the many children of Queen Anne and Prince George survived to adulthood. With no surviving children, Queen Anne was the last monarch of the Royal House of Stuart. Queen Anne style architecture and furniture was named after her 200 years later. Queen Anne's lace is named after both this Queen Anne and her great grandmother, Anne of Denmark, who was the queen consort of King James I. The lovely white flower, sometimes called an invasive weed with edible roots that smell like carrots, has been studied for its medicinal purposes.

The royal badge of Queen Anne was a crown over the entwined thistle of Scotland and the Tudor Rose of England, depicted in the Annapolis flag. She married Prince George of Denmark and Norway (Duke of Cumberland), and reigned for 12 years. One of Queen Anne's enduring contributions was building the Ascot Racecourse in 1711, located about six miles south of Windsor. It is the showplace for England's fashionable people and their impressive thoroughbred horses. The racecourse has been rebuilt several times and continues as one of the Royal properties. Queen Elizabeth II is a noted horse enthusiast and owner. Thirty-two years after Ascot was built in England, the first recorded thoroughbred horse race in North America took place in Parole.

Annapolis Flag

Sources: www.Maryland.gov; www.Britannica.com/biography

The Royal House of Stewart or Stuart

Beginnings in Scotland

Nine monarchs of the Royal House of Stewart ruled Scotland only for 232 years from 1371 to 1603. The Royal House of Stewart (Scotland) and its royal lineage intertwined with England in 1503, when Margaret Tudor, a sister of Henry VIII of England, married James IV (Stewart) of Scotland (1488-1513). The reign of their son, James V (Stewart) of Scotland, who married Madeleine of Valois (France), and upon her death married Marie de Guise of Lorraine (France), followed from1513 to 1542.

The reign of Mary, Queen of Scots, daughter of James V (Stewart) of Scotland and Marie de Guise, who married her first cousin, Henry Stuart (Lord Darnley), a descendant of both James II of Scotland and Henry VII of England, followed from 1542 to 1567. Henry Stuart was her second husband. Following an uprising against her in Scotland, she was imprisoned and forced to abdicate in favor of her one-year-old son, who became James VI of Scotland and later James I of England. After an unsuccessful attempt to regain the Scottish throne, Mary sought refuge in England to claim Elizabeth's throne. Both she and Henry Stuart were grandchildren of Margaret Tudor, sister of Henry VIII, so Mary considered herself a legitimate heir to the English throne. Elizabeth I of England considered Mary a threat and had her imprisoned for 18-1/2 years. Elizabeth then had her executed in 1587 when Mary was found guilty of plotting to assassinate Elizabeth I.

Mary, Queen of Scots, changed the spelling of the Royal House to Stuart. In 1603, her son by Henry Stuart (Lord Darnley), James VI (Stuart) of Scotland, who had ruled Scotland since 1567, assumed the additional title of James I of England. He succeeded the youngest daughter of Henry VIII, Elizabeth I, his first cousin twice removed and the last monarch of the Royal House of Tudor. His succession joined the two countries of Scotland and England. James had the possibly unwonted experience of succeeding the queen who had his mother executed.

Continuation in England
James I (reigned 1603-1625), son of Mary, Queen of Scots, and Henry Stuart (Lord Darnley), married Anne of Denmark. He was James VI of Scotland when both Scotland and England joined as one country in 1603, and he then assumed the title of James I of England.

Historical note: It was England's James I for whom the King James Version of The Holy Bible is named. The first English translation from the Hebrew and Greek was completed during the reign of Henry VIII (1539). Building on that earlier version, the 54-member committee appointed by James I took seven years to complete the second English translation. The King James Version of the Bible was first printed in 1611.

Charles I (reigned 1625-1649), son of James I and Anne of Denmark, married Queen Mary for whom Maryland is named. Charles I was executed for treason during the first English Civil War between the Parliamentarians (Roundheads) and the Royalists (Cavaliers) over the manner of England's form of governance and whether the monarchy had power over Parliament. The war involved England, Ireland, and Scotland and is sometimes called the war of the kingdoms. Two more English Civil Wars followed. Concurrently the Thirty Years' War devastated central Europe. Escaping those wars fueled much of the early migration to the British colonies of America. A portrait of Charles I astride a white horse painted around 1633 by Flemish artist Anthony van Dyck hangs in Highclere Castle located 66 miles west of London. The portrait was shown in the dining room in the Downton Abbey television series, which was filmed at Highclere Castle. The portrait can also be seen on line. Charles I and Mary's children were Charles II, Mary Henrietta (mother of William III), James II, and several more.

Lord Oliver Cromwell and his son Richard ruled for 11 years before the monarchy was restored.

Charles II (reigned 1660-1685), first son of Charles I and Queen Mary, married Catherine of Braganza (Portugal). They had no surviving children.

James II (reigned 1685-1688) second son of Charles I and Queen Mary, had two daughters, Mary and Anne (both future queens) by first wife, Anne Hyde, Duchess of York, and one son, James Edward "Old Pretender" by second wife, Mary of Modena (Italy).

Neither James Edward nor his son, Charles Edward "Young Pretender," also known as "Bonnie Prince Charlie," succeeded in regaining the British throne, mostly due to the fear of England becoming a Catholic country (James II had converted to Catholicism before becoming King). James II was deposed by William III, his nephew and son-in-law.

William III, son of William II of Orange (the Netherlands) and Mary Henrietta Stuart, eldest daughter of Charles I and Queen

Mary, was therefore a nephew of Charles II and James II. William III married his first cousin, Mary II, the first daughter of James II and Anne Hyde, which made William III also James II's son-in law. William and Mary reigned from 1689 to 1702 until Mary's death in 1694, after which William ruled as sole monarch. They had no surviving children.

Historical note: *The College of William & Mary, located in Williamsburg, Virginia, is the second-oldest institution of higher education in the United States, after Harvard University. It was founded in 1693 by King William III and Queen Mary II. Many early leaders of the United States were educated there.*

Anne (reigned 1702 – 1714), for whom Annapolis is named, was the second daughter of James II and Anne Hyde. Queen Anne had married Prince George of Denmark and Norway (Duke of Cumberland); they had no surviving children. Queen Anne was the last monarch of the Royal House of Stuart. She was succeeded by her second cousin, George I of the House of Hanover.

The National Anthem of the United Kingdom and Northern Ireland, "God Save the Queen" is available on-line, with their flag, known as the Union Jack in red and white crosses on a blue background, flying in the background. Parts of the Union Jack are reproduced in many flags of the 53 members of the British Commonwealth of Nations. The English origination of both the lyrics and the melody is obscure. America appropriated the melody and now sings the lyrics penned by Rev. Samuel Francis Smith in 1832 while he was at the Andover Theological Seminary in Newton, Massachusetts. He called his hymn "America" also known as "My Country Tis of Thee." England is remembered for its educational institutes, Shakespeare, Stonehenge, Windsor Castle, pubs, tea and its long history.

The Royal Stewart tartan (pattern) of Scotland, with its distinctive sett or pattern of criss-crossed horizontal and vertical bands of red, blue, green and white colors is the personal tartan of Queen Elizabeth II. The tartan registry, first published in1831, is reflected in clothing, pillows, throws and even biscuit tins for Scottish shortbread. Occasionally the queen has worn the Balmoral tartan, which was designed in 1853 by Queen Victoria's husband, Prince Albert. That is the only tartan which cannot be worn by anyone without the Queen's permission. The history and origins of the tartan knee-length skirt with pleats at the back is available on-line. The adventurous Celtic people, specifically the Scotti (Latin name for the Gaels) tribe of Ireland, began the tartan tradition in the fifth century and in the process gave Scotland its name. With over 50 million people claiming Scots heritage and over 25,000 registered tartans for the clans of Scotland, they are now seen all over the globe. A number of Scottish national anthems, such as "Flower of Scotland" and "Scotland the Brave" played by orchestras and bagpipes are available on-line. Some show the Scottish flag, or the Saltire, a white x-shaped cross representing Saint Andrew, the patron saint of Scotland, on a background of blue, flying during the anthems. In addition to kilts and bagpipes, Scotland is also recognized for its invention of golf and its whisky.

The somewhat official Irish kilt is made of a plain color, Saffron mustard yellow, with a complementing black jacket and scarf. They also have pale blue and green tartans, with each district or county in Ireland claiming its own tartan. Brian Boru, who lived over 1,000 years ago and subdued about 150 other kings of

Ireland in the Battle of Clontarf near the then small village of Dublin, became the High King of Ireland (1014). The entire island of Ireland (which includes the six counties of Northern Ireland, a part of the UK) is slightly smaller than Maine. Though Boru was killed immediately following the battle, he is considered the first national ruler of Ireland who managed through his children and grandchildren to unify all the former kings and assimilate the Norse (Viking) raiders into their Irish culture. The Borus begat the O'Brien clan which now claims its very own tartan. There's a Brian Boru pub and restaurant in Severna Park, Maryland. One of the oldest melodies in Ireland's repertoire is "Brian Boru's March." There's a spirited rendition by The Chieftains available on-line. He was also the subject of at least two operas. Boru is buried in St. Patrick's Cathedral Armagh near Dublin. The lyrics of Ireland's national anthem "The Soldier's Song" was originally composed in English by Peadar Kearney and the melody by Patrick Kearney in 1909 or 1910. The Irish translation was written by Liam O'Rinn in 1923. Beautiful renditions are available on-line in both languages with Ireland's new flag of vertical green, white and orange colors flying in the background. Green represents the native Irish (most of whom are Roman Catholic); orange represents the British supporters of William of Orange (the Netherlands) who settled in Northern Ireland in the 17th century (most of whom are Protestant); and the white center represents peace between the two groups. In addition to its world-famous music, Ireland is recognized for its ales and lagers, shamrocks, castles, literature, the harp and the Celtic cross.

Wales, with 37 registered tartans, all made in their country of 100% pure new wool, cannot be left behind. Wales, a bit smaller than New Jersey, boasts many entertainers, Sir George Everest (1790-1855), surveyor and geographer with the famous mountain namesake, four times more sheep than humans and more castles per square mile than anywhere else in the world. In addition, what they may lack in numbers of tartans is made up for with their popular cattle-herding dogs, the Welsh Corgis. They remain the favorite of Queen Elizabeth who has owned over 30 of them. There are renditions available on-line of the rousing Welsh National Anthem, "Land of My Fathers" sung in both Welsh and English, also with the Welsh flag flying – a heraldic red dragon on a green (bottom) and white (top) background, the only part of the UK not represented on the Union Jack. The size of the United Kingdom (Scotland, England, Wales and afore-mentioned Northern Ireland) is about the same as the combination of Virginia and North Carolina.

Many citizens residing in the 53 British Commonwealth countries wear kilts. Other countries also wearing kilts: Spain, Germany, Egypt, France, Greece and the United States, to name a few. The tradition has circulated around the world!

Sources: Kings and Queens of England wall chart; www.Britannica.com/HouseofStuart

Maryland Census of 1860 and 2010

Maryland Census of 1860

This last census taken prior to the Civil War reveals the following about the population of the state of Maryland

Maryland's population totaled 687,049, of whom 83,942 were free blacks.

Maryland's enslaved population totaled 87,189.

In Anne Arundel County, there were 4,864 free blacks and 7,332 enslaved.

85,000 Marylanders enlisted during the Civil War: 77% fought for the Union, and the remainder for the Confederacy.

Maryland Census of 2010

The census taken 150 years later reveals the following about the population of the state of Maryland:

Maryland's population totaled 5,773,562, with the following breakdown

White: 3,359,284

African-American: 1,700,298

Asian: 318,853

American Indian and Alaska Native: 20,420

Native Hawaiian and Pacific Islander: 3,157

Other: 206,832

Identified by two or more: 164,708

Sources: U.S. Census Bureau; Maryland Census Data

The Terrible Cost of the Civil War

Though the North and the South both suffered catastrophic losses during the four years of conflict, property devastation was far greater south of the Mason-Dixon line. The British team of Charles Mason (astronomer) and Jeremiah Dixon (surveyor) were commissioned to survey the land between 1763 and 1767 to resolve a border dispute between the British colonies of Maryland, Pennsylvania, and Delaware, due to the confusing and overlapping royal charters. The survey was mainly to settle a family feud between the sons of William Penn and the Calvert family. The surveyed line runs between Pennsylvania and Maryland and part of West Virginia, originally part of Virginia, and drops south to carve out what became the state of Delaware (the first state). Several historical and fictional books have been written about the history of how the Mason-Dixon border was created.

The following are some gruesome statistics from the Civil War:
- 25% of Southern white men of military age were killed.
- 25% of all Southerners who fought were permanently injured.
- 20% of Mississippi's revenue in 1866 was earmarked for the purchase of artificial limbs.
- At the Battle of Gettysburg alone, there were up to 51,000 Confederate and Union casualties.
- More than 25% of Union soldiers were killed or wounded.
- 40,000 black soldiers died, 30,000 from wounds and disease.
- 80 Confederate and 80 Union generals were killed.
- Two regiments, the 1st Texas (at Antietam) and the 1st Minnesota (at Gettysburg), lost 82% of their men in a single

battle.

- 500,000 farms and plantations in the South were destroyed during the war or became insolvent.

- By the end of the war, more than 60% of Southern-based railroad companies were bankrupt, and most rail lines were unfit for use.

- In Columbia, S.C., 1,386 buildings were destroyed or burned.

- 66% of all assessed wealth in the South was lost.

- The combined cost of the war for both the Union and Confederacy was $81 billion.

Sources:
Historical Times Encyclopedia of the Civil War,
The Civil War Book of Lists
Congressional Research Service

President Abraham Lincoln: His Family and His Legacy

President Abraham Lincoln (1809-1865) and his wife Mary Todd Lincoln (1818-1882) had four children: Robert Todd Lincoln (1843-1926), Edward "Eddie" Baker Lincoln (1846-1850), William "Willie" Wallace Lincoln (1850-1862), and Thomas "Tad" Lincoln (1853-1871).

Abraham Lincoln

President Lincoln and His Family in Illinois, Kentucky, and Washington, D.C.

Abraham Lincoln served one term representing a central Illinois Congressional District in the U.S. House of Representatives, 30th Congress, from 1847 to 1849. That district was later represented by Rep. Everett Dirksen, who later became a Senator, and Rep. Robert H. Michel who rose to become House Minority Leader.

Mary Todd Lincoln

Mary and their two sons, Robert and Eddie, accompanied Lincoln to Washington for his first and only Congressional term. It was an arduous journey via stagecoach and railroad through Kentucky to visit the Todd family on their way to Washington. That was their first experience with taking the railroad into Washington. The two children and Mary soon went to live with her stepmother in Kentucky until the end of his term. The cornerstone of the Washington Monument, a tribute to our first President, was laid on July 4, 1848. Lincoln witnessed the ceremony. The Lincolns all returned to Illinois after his term was completed. Lincoln returned to Illinois politics and the practice of law throughout the eighth judicial district. In March of 1850, just before turning four, their second son Eddie died from tuberculosis. Their third son Willie was born in late 1850 and their fourth son Thomas "Tad" in 1853.

After his November 6, 1860, election to the presidency, just prior to his inauguration and under heavy guard due to security threats, newly elected President Lincoln, his wife Mary, and their three surviving sons took the train from Springfield, Illinois, into the New Jersey and C Street station in Washington and then headed to their new home at the White House. The family did not return home to Illinois for the entire time of his presidency due to the Civil War.

Lincoln was inaugurated on March 4, 1861, sworn in by the 5th Chief Justice of the Supreme Court, Roger B. Taney, who will forever be remembered for the infamous *Dred Scott* decision. Taney was from Maryland and a brother-in-law to Francis Scott Key.

Five weeks after Lincoln's swearing-in, on April 12, the Civil War began at Fort Sumter, South Carolina. In 1862, at the age of 12, his son Willie died of typhoid fever while the family lived in the White House. He was buried in the Georgetown section of Washington and later reburied in the Lincoln family plot in Illinois.

Lincoln was reelected to a second term in November of 1864 while the war continued. On March 4, 1865, he was sworn in by the 6th

Chief Justice of the Supreme Court, Salmon P. Chase, The war had still not ended. Chief Justice Chase had served as Secretary of the Treasury for Lincoln's first term and managed to keep the country solvent while prosecuting the war. Upon the death of Roger B. Taney, ironically the same day Maryland abolished slavery, Lincoln nominated Chase to fill the vacancy for Chief Justice of the Supreme Court.

On April 9, 1865, at Appomattox Court House in central Virginia, Confederate General Robert E. Lee surrendered his army to Union General Ulysses S. Grant, effectively ending the Civil War, just short of four years after the fighting began. On April 11, Lincoln made his last public speech to a throng of citizens who had gathered outside the White House to celebrate the end of the Civil War. He focused on the problems the country could expect to face during reconstruction after the war. The speech is available on line.

Only 40 days after his second swearing-in, on April 15, 1865, Lincoln met his untimely end from an assassin, Marylander John Wilkes Booth, at Ford's Theater, located near the White House. Lincoln, the first U.S. president to be assassinated, was 56 years old.

President Lincoln's death came less than a week after the Confederacy had surrendered in Virginia, with one Captain Robert Todd Lincoln in attendance in his capacity as a member of General Ulysses Grant's staff.

The Civil War, though nothing about it was remotely "civil," pulled the country apart, and the republic barely survived the ordeal. It has been estimated that 620,000 soldiers from both sides of the conflict died during that miserable four years. Thousands more were wounded. Many books have been written and continue being written about the conflict.

Abraham Lincoln gave his all to heal the country's divisions. Lincoln's life had ended, with so little time to recover from the strain of his entire presidency being consumed by civil war, the loss of a second child during their time in the White House, and the effect of the war on his family. After his death, there would be no opportunity for the president to grow old with his wife and remaining two sons. As Edwin Stanton, Lincoln's Secretary of War during the Civil War said at the time of his death, "Now he belongs to the ages." And so he does.

Sidebar: The controversial *Dred Scott* Supreme Court decision of 1857 was a crucial case in this country's history of slavery. For years historians have discussed Dred Scott and his family's lives, their long legal battle to attain freedom, and the role of the Supreme Court decision in the lead-up to the Civil War. The Supreme Court ruled that Americans of African descent, whether free or enslaved, were not American citizens and therefore could not sue in federal court. The Court also ruled that Congress lacked power to ban slavery in the U.S. territories. The end of the Civil War, the abolition of slavery, and the ratification on July 28, 1868 of the 14th Amendment to the Constitution granting citizenship to all persons born or naturalized in the United States, which included former slaves, essentially overruled the *Dred Scott* decision.

Sources: Lincoln biographies and historical annals; Ford's Theatre Museum, Washington, D.C.; Dirksen Center in Illinois; *Dred Scott v. Sandford*, 60 U.S. (19 How.) 393 (1857)

President Lincoln's Legislative Legacy

U.S. Department of Agriculture: In 1862, President Abraham Lincoln started the U.S. Department of Agriculture.

The Emancipation Proclamation: Issued by President Lincoln on January 1, 1863, the act freed only the enslaved living in the eleven states in open rebellion against the union. Maryland, one of four border states, did not free its enslaved until November 1, 1864, 22 months later, and only a few months before Congress approved the 13th Amendment to the Constitution abolishing slavery throughout the United States.

It is not only the Emancipation Proclamation freeing the enslaved in states in rebellion and holding the Union together for which Lincoln is remembered. He also signed into law three acts that would greatly define post-Civil War America.

The Homestead Act: It was signed in May of 1862, allowing any American, including the formerly enslaved, to put in a claim for up to 160 acres of federal land. By the end of the Civil War, 15,000 homestead claims had been established, with more following in the postwar years. Eventually 1.6 million individual claims would be approved, giving away 420,000 square miles of territory.

The Pacific Railway Act: Signed by Lincoln in July of 1862, authorizing the Union Pacific Railroad and Central Pacific Railroad to build a railroad and telegraph line from Omaha, Nebraska, to Sacramento, California.

The Morrill Act: Also signed in July of 1862, this act was named after then Representative and later Senator Justin Smith Morrill of

Vermont. The Morrill Act created the land-grant college system in America, focusing on agriculture, engineering, without excluding other scientific and classical studies, and military tactics. The amount of land given to land-grant colleges totaled 17,400,000 acres. Ultimately 106 colleges in the United States were founded as land-grant colleges. Many of the above colleges have a Morrill Hall on their campus, including the University of Maryland.

Source: biography.your.dictionary.com/articles/abrahamlincoln/accomplishments.html

The Lincoln Family Post Civil War
Kentucky had been one of four "border" states that did not secede from the union. Maryland, Delaware, and Missouri were the other three, with West Virginia, formed from western Virginia on June 20, 1863, making up the fifth border state. When West Virginia was carved out of Virginia, care was taken to include the eastern panhandle within the new state to ensure that the railroad remained within states either neutral or under Northern control. Many citizens in border states fought on both sides, brothers against brothers and families against families.

Kentucky-born Mary Todd Lincoln was just shy of seven when her mother died; her father remarried and had another family. Her brother served in the Confederacy as a surgeon. She lost two of her half-brothers and a brother-in-law in battle; and another half-brother was wounded in the war. Most of her family supported the Confederacy. Her life was continually filled with grief for the losses in her family.

Robert Todd Lincoln had arrived back at the White House

sometime during the five days between the South's surrender and the assassination of his father. In conversations during that short time, his father suggested Robert lay aside his uniform and return to college to read law. He did both. He resigned his military commission, moved to Chicago to study and practice law, married Mary Harlan, daughter of a U.S. Senator from Iowa, raised a family and served his country in several capacities.

Following Lincoln's state funeral, the president's remains and those of his son Willie, exhumed from the cemetery in the Georgetown section of Washington, accompanied by their mother, Mary Todd Lincoln and her two surviving sons, Robert and Tad, began the eight-day journey back to their home in Springfield, Illinois. The funeral train left from that same railroad station in Washington where the family had arrived four years earlier. Maryland was the first state the funeral train traveled through. The train traveled through 180 cities or towns and seven states before arriving in Illinois.

After Abraham Lincoln's funeral, the family settled in Chicago while Robert Todd Lincoln continued the study and practice of law. Mary and Tad moved to Europe for several years. Thomas (Tad), fourth and youngest son of President and Mrs. Lincoln, who was 12 when the family left the White House, died in 1871, at age 18, probably from tuberculosis. He and his mother had recently returned to Chicago from Europe. Tad's funeral was held at Robert's home in Chicago. Robert accompanied Tad's coffin on the train from Chicago to Springfield, Illinois, but their mother Mary Todd Lincoln was too distraught to make the trip. She lived another 11 years, mostly with a sister in Springfield, Illinois, often physically and mentally ill. She died in 1882 at 63, 17 years after the death of her husband.

Abraham and Mary Todd Lincoln and three of their children—Eddie, Willie, and Tad—are buried in the Lincoln crypt in Oak Ridge Cemetery, Springfield, Illinois.

Robert Todd Lincoln, who had served on General Ulysses Grant's staff after graduating from Harvard, studied and practiced law in Chicago, served in executive, cabinet, and ambassadorial positions, and held a long-standing leadership position with the Pullman Palace Car Company.

The Harlan-Lincoln House, built in 1876 and used as a summer home during Robert and Mary Harlan Lincoln's early married life, still stands today in Mt. Pleasant, Iowa. Mary Harlan Lincoln inherited the home from her father, Senator James Harlan, who had also served as president of Iowa Wesleyan College. The Harlan-Lincoln House now serves as a museum with artifacts from the Harlan and Lincoln families.

Robert Todd Lincoln's last public appearance was on May 30, 1922, at the dedication of the Lincoln Memorial on the National Mall in Washington, D.C. Several books have been written about his life. He lived to be almost 83 and died at the family's newer summer home, Hildene, in Manchester, Vermont, in 1926. Hildene, a Georgian Revival mansion, was built in 1905. The home was open

Robert Todd Lincoln

only to Lincoln descendants until 1975. The estate is now open to the public, along with 13 historic buildings, 400 acres of farmland, horses, goats, cows, a cheese factory, historic gardens, and vintage Pullman railroad cars. Pictures of the Hildene estate are available on line.

Mary Harlan Lincoln died in Washington at the age of 90, almost 11 years after her husband died. Robert Todd Lincoln, Mary Harlan Lincoln, and their son Abraham Lincoln II (whose remains were disinterred in Illinois and re-interred in the family tomb) are buried at Arlington National Cemetery in Arlington, Virginia. Ironically, Arlington National Cemetery is on land that was once the plantation of the family of Robert E. Lee who led the Confederate forces against the Union during the Civil War.

Robert Todd and Mary Harlan Lincoln had three children and three grandchildren. Their only son, Abraham "Jack" Lincoln II died at 16 from blood poisoning.

Their daughter Mary "Mamie" Lincoln married Charles Isham, and they had a son, Lincoln Isham, who married Leahalma Correa. Lincoln Isham became a stepfather to Leahalma's daughter Frances Mantley, but Lincoln and Leahalma Isham had no children.

Their second daughter Jessie Harlan Lincoln married Warren Beckwith. The Beckwiths had two children, Mary Lincoln "Peggy" Beckwith and Robert Todd Lincoln Beckwith, neither of whom had children.

The direct Lincoln family line died out in 1985 with the death of Robert Todd Lincoln Beckwith, great-grandson of Abraham and

Mary Todd Lincoln, grandson of Robert Todd Lincoln and Mary Harlan Lincoln, and son of Jessie Harlan Lincoln and Warren Beckwith.

Many Lincoln family pictures can be seen on-line.

Source: Lincoln stories collected by Joyce Edelson

Part III: Parole Rotary Club

Rotary Club of Parole (Annapolis) Maryland, Inc.

The Rotary Club of Parole, informally known as the Parole Rotary Club, would like to tell you who we are, what we have done, and what we are doing. We also extend to you an invitation to join us with your energy and new ideas. Our website is www.parole-rotary.org.

History of the Rotary Club

The first Rotary Club in the world was begun by Paul Harris, an attorney from Chicago, who gathered three business associates together on February 23. 1905. The organization began as a social organization for local professionals but quickly grew into a service club. There are now 35,533 clubs in over 200 countries and 1.2 million Rotarians in the world. The stated purpose of Rotary is to bring business and professional leaders together to provide humanitarian service, encourage high ethical standards in all vocations, and advance good will and peace throughout the world. To learn more about Rotary International and their service projects, visit their website: www.rotary.org.

Rotary Motto: Service above Self

Rotary is divided into districts. Our district 7620 includes 60 different Rotary clubs in central Maryland and the District of Columbia. The Rotary Club of Parole (Annapolis) was chartered on December 10, 1985. We were sponsored by the Annapolis Rotary Club under the guidance of George Benson, known affectionately as our Godfather. There were 31 charter members, some of whom are still active.

Here is a message from our president: "We are leaders in our community and are one of the most active and vibrant service clubs in our Rotary District. Our members are professionals who enthusiastically share and demonstrate the Rotary philosophy. We provide support for vocational and career development. We also have fun. Through our support of a wide range of causes, we provide hands-on volunteer opportunities with a direct impact on our local, national and international community. The Parole Rotary Club has awarded over $645,000 in local community grants and donated more than $725,000 to the Rotary International Foundation to fund community projects all over the world. Membership in our club provides an opportunity to become connected with others in addressing community needs, and interacts with local professionals, government leaders and schools. I welcome you to explore our website (www.parole-rotary.org) to learn about Rotary, upcoming events, activities, and how to apply for club membership. We meet every Tuesday morning, 7:30 a.m. at the Double Tree Hotel at 210 Holiday Court, Annapolis, off Riva Road in Parole. We would be happy to have you as our guest and even happier to have you as a member! We are always looking for new ideas for service projects and new members who share our desire to help others in our community and around the world. Please feel free to contact us today for further information."

Projects of the Parole Rotary Club
We created a ball field at the then new Annapolis High School that had been relocated to Riva Road. It took 600 truckloads of fill dirt, 13,000 square feet of sod, and cost $11,000.

We contribute time, ability, and talent to Habitat for Humanity and Christmas in April to build and refurbish houses for the elderly and disabled, highway adoption, and charity golf tournaments—all to raise the profile of Rotary and funds for community projects.

We have participated in the Rotary Youth Exchange for nine years, hosting students to and from Spain, Germany, Hungary, Romania, Italy, Sardinia, Brazil, Chile, and Taiwan.

Our club continues partnership with Polio Plus, a Rotary International effort. The world is within striking distance of having polio completely eradicated from the earth. Currently only three countries have active cases of polio.

We participate in the Salvation Army Christmastime bell-ringing, Homeless Resource Day, and TREEmendous tree planting at local schools and neighborhoods.

We have an active scholarship endowment at Anne Arundel Community College.

We sponsor an active Interact Club at Broadneck High School in Anne Arundel County. The club received an award for the most bikes collected to be sent all over the world. These dedicated and energetic students represent the future of Rotary. The Interact Club sponsors a 4-way speech contest, which is held at Broadneck High School; prizes are given for the top three winners. The students select a current issue of interest to them and make a presentation using Rotary's 4-way test to foster the principles of ethics in everyday life and in one's profession.

We participate in presenting Rotary Youth Leadership Awards (RYLA) each year. RYLA is an intense three-day training program designed to recognize, encourage, and further develop leadership, problem-solving and communication skills of high school students in grades 10, 11, and 12. Inspirational speakers, community leaders, and peer mentors discuss how to turn motivation into action and form lasting friendships. District 7620 organizes this conference over President's Day weekend in February. Several hundred students from all over the district are invited to attend. Applications are made on line. All costs except transportation are paid by Rotary. Our club has traditionally sponsored six to eight students every year. The nearest Rotary Club can provide details. Previous participants have been unanimous in their praise of the RYLA program.

Every year we give away dictionaries to third graders in six local schools.

We participate in activities of the Light House Shelter for the Homeless through donations to help provide services, and have used their catering services for Rotary events. (See article in this book on the Light House Shelter and the new Light House Bistro at their former West Street location.)

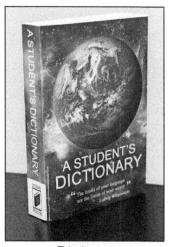

Dictionary
Image courtesy of Les Howard Studios

We support the Safe Blood Program, where our donations are used mostly in education internationally to help people understand the importance of safe blood in their lives.

Under our Navy home football parking project, we direct vehicular traffic for all home football games played at the Navy

Marine Corps Memorial Stadium. All volunteers are invited to attend our tailgate once the game starts. The Naval Academy Athletic Association (NAAA), which owns the stadium, contracts with our club to provide needed parking services. The funds paid to our Rotary club for our services are distributed into our community through a grants program. (See article in this book on the Naval Academy.) In addition, in late January, our members donate their time and brave the cold to help direct parking at the stadium for participants in the Polar Bear Plunge at Sandy Point State Park, near the Chesapeake Bay Bridge, which raises funds for Special Olympics.

Parole Rotary Club members who direct parking for Gate 2, one of eight gates covered by members of the Parole Rotary Club during home Navy games

Our club provided funds to build a greenhouse at the Phoenix Academy, 1411 Cedar Park Road, Annapolis (near the Navy Marine Corps Memorial Stadium). The greenhouse at Phoenix Academy has been a much needed and appreciated addition to the school farm. Phoenix is one of three schools in Anne Arundel County that offers an agriculture program as part of the Career and Technical Education Department. The greenhouse is essential for the agriculture curriculum to be taught as a hands-on class throughout the school year. Students who are

Greenhouse
Image courtesy of Les Howard Studios

Phoenix Academy
Image courtesy of Les Howard Studios

less comfortable with other aspects of farming often are more comfortable in the greenhouse setting, making the program more inclusive and welcoming. This new climate-controlled structure has also allowed the inclusion of modern farming techniques such as hydroponics and aquaponics, giving staff the opportunity to prepare students for meaningful and promising career choices. Plants grown within the greenhouse have been sold to teachers and other staff to help build connections to the program across the school. As the facility is being completed, plans are in the works for public plant sales to raise ongoing funds for the program. Thanks to the generosity of the Parole Rotary Club, the Phoenix Academy has been able to add much needed storage structures.

Our club mentored and supported two club presidents who later became Rotary District Governors: John Murkey and Bill Fine.

Books for International Goodwill (B.I.G.), under the leadership of Steve Frantzich, has processed over eight million books and has contributed textbooks and other books to build community and school libraries all over the world. In our own country, B.I.G. has provided books to Native American Reservation libraries and to under-funded inner-city school libraries. Locally B.I.G. has held periodic book sales—at reduced rates for teachers—and the community. B.I.G. has received many awards. (See article in this book on B.I.G.) The B.I.G. website is www.big-books.org.

Parole Rotary Club's Mission

We are a service club that significantly improves lives in our local community and around the world by meeting real needs.

Parole Rotary Club's Vision

We will make a positive difference for youth today, so they will make a difference tomorrow.

Meetings include fellowship, a generous breakfast and an interesting program. Subjects range from our community to professional development, the arts, the media, international affairs, environment, politics, education, and more.

If your desire is to join an organization that has many opportunities for service, you have found the right club. We are a very active club that does a lot for the community. There are many ways to get involved and you will get to know a lot of exceptional people.

Written by members of the Parole Rotary Club

BOOKS FOR INTERNATIONAL GOODWILL (B.I.G.): A BIG PROJECT

Few would have expected that Parole Rotary Club's sponsorship of a foreign student from South Africa would lead to a signature project to improve literacy in more than 20 countries. On her arrival back home, the student sent a plaintive letter outlining some good news and some bad news. On the good news side, she had been named the principal of two high schools. On the bad news side, neither school had adequate books to educate their pupils. Leonard Blackshear and other club members sprang into action, gathering thousands of books from the Anne Arundel County school system and other sources.

BIG
Image courtesy of Les Howard Studios

Thus began Books for International Goodwill (B.I.G.) in 1999. In the early years, it was a slow process to gather the 20,000 books needed to fill a container, and it was agonizing work to load over 500 boxes of books per container by hand. Money was tight and volunteers limited.

Finding a successive set of affordable locations for the operation became a constant battle as the organization moved six times in 18 years. Each move required significant effort dismantling shelves and packing up thousands of books.

A well-oiled operation requires a usable warehouse space, adequate incoming books, manpower to sort and pack books, the identification of recipients, and the financial resources to cover costs. Each time one of the demands was met, another would crop up. Despite the challenges, B.I.G. prevailed in its mission of "keeping books alive."

During its tenure, B.I.G. has processed over eight million books, with a solid core of over 30 volunteers, supplemented by an influx of volunteers from organizations such as the Naval Academy's Midshipman Action Group and the Single Volunteers of Baltimore. B.I.G. has received commendations from the Points of Light Foundation, the Maryland State government, and the Anne Arundel County Arts Council. More importantly, it has placed millions of books in the hands of under-served populations both internationally and domestically. In the process, it has saved thousands of cubic feet of landfill space into which many of the books would have been destined. B.I.G. is a win-win operation. Those who donate books realize their books can help others. Volunteers have a sense of accomplishment, and recipients receive the resources they need to improve literacy. The periodic book sales that largely fund the operation provide books at reasonable prices. We believe that B.I.G. is the largest volunteer-based book distribution project in the world. Not far from the Parole community, a great deal is going on. You can check out B.I.G. at www.big-books.org. Our new location: 451 Defense Highway on Maryland Route 450 (about two miles west of Annapolis Mall).

Source: Steve Frantzich, Rotarian, President of B.I.G., and retired U.S. Naval Academy Professor

Naptown barBAYq Contest and Music Festival

In late 2009, a number of members of the Parole Rotary Club, led by Don Chomas and Bill Fine, discussed the idea for a barbeque contest sanctioned by the Kansas City Barbeque Society (KCBS), the largest barbeque sanctioning body in the country. For a fee, food vendors, crafters, and other merchants would be offered space to sell their wares. Local bands and music acts would be offered a venue to showcase their talents. Cash prizes would be awarded to winning contestants in a contest governed by the rules set out by KCBS and under the oversight of KCBS officials. After considerable investigation and planning, it was decided that the first event would be held the first weekend in May of 2011. It took a full year of planning to get everything done to host the event. A venue was secured at the Navy Marine Corps Memorial Stadium in Annapolis, and the event was announced through KCBS publications and website. The event was held on Friday May 6, and Saturday May 7, 2011. While not successful financially, it was apparent that the potential for raising funds was good in future years.

Taking the lessons learned from that first event, planning started for the second annual Naptown barBAYq Contest and Music Festival in June of 2011. The dates of the first weekend in May 2012 seemed good, but the venue needed to be changed. The decision was made to move the event to the Anne Arundel County Fairgrounds in Crownsville where there was more room and better infrastructure for the event. It also allowed for an admission charge to the event which would greatly improve the bottom line and was not possible at the stadium. That second event allowed more contestant teams for the contest and more vendors and merchants. That event was more successful financially and showed the potential for substantial fund-raising.

Subsequent years saw an increase in size and scope of the event and an increase in funds raised. Committees planning and coordinating the event became more structured and procedures more defined, but it was still a year-long planning effort. The greatest risk was weather and there was no way to adequately mitigate it. The sixth year, 2016, saw a rainy weekend with very low attendance. The committee decided that the amount of work and planning to produce the event was far too great for the risk of another bad year. Over the six years, the club earned enough to provide over $120,000 in grants to local organizations supporting youth welfare and health.

The Rotary Club was approached in the early fall of 2016 by ABC Events, Inc., with an inquiry to purchase the event for their portfolio. ABC Events produces several events in the Annapolis area, including the Maryland Seafood Festival, the Maryland Chicken Wing Festival, and the Bay Bridge Paddle. Negotiations were completed and ABC Events now owns and produces the Naptown barBAYq Contest. All of their events feature a non-profit component and the Parole Rotary Club remains affiliated

Father and child enjoying the Naptown barBAYq
Image courtesy of Les Howard Studios

with them and the Naptown barBAYq by providing volunteers for the event. In return, the club receives a share of the net proceeds. The website www.barbayq.com has the latest news of the event. Note: ABC Events, Inc. has since suspended the event.

This is just one example of the power of Rotary, and the Parole Rotary Club in particular, to make a difference in our community by raising funds for grants to local nonprofits supporting youth-related programs.

Source: Henry Riser, Past President (twice) of Parole Rotary Club and barBAYq Chair

Closing

This ends our delightful adventure with the citizens and historical neighborhood of Greater Parole. The courage, stamina, and spirit of Parole's residents, past and present, have made the experience enlightening and enjoyable. We hope everyone has enjoyed reading about this neighborhood and its citizens as much as we did in gathering these stories. We endeavored to present Parole within its local, state, and national context. We tried to be as accurate as we could in interpreting the available research and respectful of our neighbors in Parole who shared their lives. The legacy of those who have been a part of Parole's history will long be remembered and honored through oral and written histories. Any errors were inadvertent and we ask your understanding of the effort and dedication to the process of sharing citizens' experiences for this book, and to please forgive any trespasses. Please feel free to share your thoughts with the editor.

The journey doesn't end here; please stay in touch with us and continue to share additional Parole memories and history with the editor, Joyce Edelson. She can be reached via e- mail at JoyceEdelson@gmail.com.

Thank you to all who participated and for purchasing this book, the proceeds of which will further the community service goals of the Parole Rotary Club (www.parole-rotary.org).

Yours in Rotary,
Members of the Parole Rotary Club

Please see some of our favorite recipes on the following pages.

Appendix: Favorite Recipes from the Rotary Club

Traditional Maryland Recipes

Maryland is known for its seafood, especially its crabs and oysters, but also is famous for other dishes traditional to southern Maryland.

Southern Maryland Stuffed Ham

Legends abound about the origination of Southern Maryland Stuffed Ham. A plausible one is that the best parts of the hogs were saved for the slave owners. The jaw bone was given to the slaves. Those pockets in the bone were stuffed with greens such as cabbage, turnip greens, kale, dandelions, sprouts, onions, peppers and all sorts of spices, to make the contents of the dish stretch as far as possible.

7-10 lb. ham (use corned bone-in ham for that authentic Southern Maryland taste)
1 head cabbage   2 lbs. kale   1 lb. onions
1 bunch scallions   1 tbsp. red pepper   2 tbsp. mustard seed
2 tbsp. celery seed   1 tsp. Tabasco sauce 2-1/2 tbsp. salt
3 tsp. ground red pepper   Cheesecloth or old pillow case

Chop onions and greens. Mix seasonings with greens. Cut 2-inch slits (pockets) on a 45-degree angle in the ham. Alternate 3 pockets then 2 pockets, making sure they are not parallel. Press seasoned stuffing into slits until they will hold no more. Put ham in cheesecloth or pillow case; add leftover stuffing and tie closed. Put ham in large pot and cover with water. Simmer or boil slowly for 20 minutes per pound or until internal temperature reaches 160°. Reduce cooking time by 1/2 hour when using precooked ham. Turn off heat. Let ham cool in the water (about 2 hours). Remove and drain. Chill ham in its cloth in refrigerator overnight. Serve cold.

By Mike Mullins, Rotarian and Rodney Dangerfield impersonator

Southern Maryland Fried Oysters

1 cup self-rising cornmeal
1 cup self-rising flour
1/4 tsp. cayenne pepper, to taste
2 eggs
2 Tbsp. milk
2 12-ounce containers of fresh oysters, drained
Vegetable oil

In a mixing bowl, add the first 3 ingredients; stir to combine. In another bowl, combine the egg and milk; whisk to combine. Dip oysters in egg mixture and then dredge in flour mixture. Add oil to 2-3 inch depth in a cast-iron Dutch oven; heat to 375°. Fry oysters in oil until golden, turning once. Drain on paper towels and serve immediately.

By Mike Mullins, Rotarian and Rodney Dangerfield impersonator

Maryland Oyster Stew

Maryland oyster stew is one of those dishes for which this state is justly famous.

Drain 1-1/2 dozen shelled large oysters in a wire strainer; retain liquid. Be sure no bits of shell lurk among them. Measure the liquor (liquid from the oyster shells) to get 1 cup; bring the liquor to a boil and remove the scum. Add 1 cup of milk. When all this comes to a boil, add the oysters and salt and pepper to taste. Cook gently, just two minutes, until oysters curl. Serve immediately, topping each bowlful with a dab of salted shipped cream.

By Ronald Lewis, Rotary supporter from Virginia

Rockfish

Best cooked in cast iron.

Preheat oven AND pan in 450° oven. Soak rockfish in milk for 10 minutes. Dry well. Put a knob of butter and a spoonful of olive oil in hot pan. Throw in fish. Cook until just flaky, about 5 minutes for a medium fillet. Remove from oven. Squeeze a half a lemon over and add salt and pepper. Slather with good mayonnaise; you can mix a little Dijon mustard with mayonnaise for a change. Serve with lemon and parsley for garnish.

By Roz Dove, mental health advocate

Crab Cakes

1 lb. crab meat (backfin or lump preferred)

Mix following ingredients in a bowl:
2 Tbsp. mayonnaise	1 egg, beaten
1/2 tsp. salt	1/2 tsp. dry mustard
Dash Worcestershire sauce	Dash tabasco sauce
1 tsp. lemon juice	1 tsp. Old Bay seasoning
6 crackers, crushed (no bread)	

Add crab meat to the above mixture. Turn together with your hands, gently to avoid breaking the crab lumps. Make into slightly flattened cakes. Coat lightly with butter. Cook in oven or under broiler until light brown on top.

By Jane Matanzo, Rotary supporter

Londontown Terrace Crab Pie

3 Tbsp. butter

1/2 cup chopped celery

1-1/2 cups shredded cheese (sharp, cheddar or swiss)

1 cup sliced onion rings

1 cup crabmeat

9-inch unbaked pastry shell

Sauté the onion rings and celery in butter until onion is soft and golden. Spoon alternate layers of crab, cheese and onion-celery mix into pie shell.

Combine in a bowl:

3 eggs

1 tsp. salt

2/3 cup half-and-half cream

1/2 tsp. pepper

Pinch of red pepper (coarse grind)

Beat together eggs, cream, salt, and pepper. Pour into pastry shell over other ingredients. Bake in hot oven (400°) until firm, about 30 to 40 minutes. When knife point inserted in center comes out clean, filling is set. Decorate with tomato wedges or cherry tomatoes, if desired. Cool slightly before cutting.

By Lynn Russack, Rotary supporter from Maryland

Carrot Fritters

Serves 8

2 Tbsp. plain flour
2 tsp. ground cumin
1 clove garlic, crushed
2 Tbsp. chopped flat-leaf parsley
3 green onions, thinly sliced
2 eggs, lightly beaten
3 carrots, peeled
2 Tbsp. olive oil
2 green onions, extra, thinly sliced lengthwise

Combine flour, cumin, garlic, parsley and green onions in large bowl. Add eggs. Mix well to combine. Coarsely grate carrots. Use your hands to squeeze out as much excess moisture as possible. Add carrots to egg mixture. Season with salt and pepper. Heat oil in non-stick frying pan over medium heat. Add ½ cup of batter per fritter to frying pan. Cook fritters in batches for 3 minutes each side, or until golden and cooked through.

By Logan and Will Hottle, Rotarian family and volunteers at Historic London Town and Gardens

Old Time Roast Wild Duck

Place duck on rack in dripping pan, sprinkle with salt and pepper, and cover breast with very thin slices of salt pork or bacon. Bake 20 to 30 minutes in a very hot oven, basting every five minutes with fat in pan. Turn duck over, lower heat, and roast until tender.

Serve with orange sauce:
1/4 cup butter
1-1/3 cups brown stock
1/4 cup flour
1/2 tsp. salt
Juice of two oranges
2 Tbsp. sherry wine
Ground rind of 1 orange

Brown the butter, add flour and salt and stir until well browned. Add stock gradually. Just before serving, add orange juice, sherry, and pieces of rind.

By Martha Lostrom, Rotarian from Kent Island

Recipes Using Fresh Produce

The garden produce of Maryland farms and gardens equals no other. A weekend is incomplete without at least one trip to a farmer's market during our beautiful summers and autumns.

Squash Casserole

2 grated carrots
2 lbs. yellow squash, sliced
1/4 cup chopped onion.
1 can cream of chicken soup
1 cup dairy sour cream
1 cup grated cheddar cheese
1 8-oz. pkg. herb seasoned stuffing mix
1/2 cup butter or margarine, melted

In saucepan in salted water, cook squash, onions, and carrots for 5 minutes. Drain well and set aside. Combine soup and sour cream and stir in cheese. Fold into well-drained squash, onions, and carrots. Combine stuffing mix with butter. Spread half of stuffing mix in bottom of 12 x 7 x 2 baking dish. Spoon vegetable mix on top. Place remainder of stuffing mix on top. Bake at 350° for 25 to 30 minutes.

By June Bartley, Rotary supporter from Virginia

Tomato Casserole

4 slices bacon

1 small onion, chopped

1-1/2 lbs. fresh tomatoes (can substitute 1 lb., 12-oz. can chopped tomatoes)

4-5 slices firm white bread, cubed

1/2 cup brown sugar

1/2 tsp. tarragon

1/2 tsp. basil

1/4 tsp. garlic powder

Salt and pepper

Parmesan cheese

Fry bacon and drain. Sauté chopped onion in bacon fat until limp. Chop tomatoes and place in 1-1/2 quart casserole. Stir in break cubes, onion, brown sugar, spices. Bake at 350° for 20 minutes. Sprinkle with Parmesan cheese and crumbled bacon and bake 10 minutes more.

By Joyce Edelson, Past President, Parole Rotary Club

Meatball and Vegetable Casserole

2 lbs. ground beef (can use 1 lb. ground sausage for one of the two lbs.)

2 eggs, slightly beaten

1 cup soft bread crumbs

1 can applesauce

1 tsp. salt if desired; or use meat seasonings (which usually contain salt)

1/4 tsp. ground pepper

1 10-1/2 oz. can tomato or mushroom soup

1 small can of mushrooms, chopped

1/2 cup water or liquid from mushrooms

1 onion, chopped

1/2 cup chopped carrots

1/2 cup chopped celery

1 chopped green pepper

Combine beef, eggs, bread crumbs, applesauce, and salt and pepper; mix lightly. Shape into 3-inch balls (no need to brown first). Arrange in 3-quart casserole. Blend together soup and water; stir vegetables into soup mix. Pour mixture over meat balls. Add different green herbs to top of casserole. Bake 1 hour at 350-375°. Let cool for a bit before serving so the meatballs can absorb the liquid.

By Vivian Dinges, Rotary supporter from Virginia

Gazpacho

This is a seasonal soup, sometimes called "a liquid salad," best made with ripe tomatoes and seasoned with fresh basil. I use a hand-held blender to liquefy the ingredients and serve garnished with a basil leaf and/or croutons. The optional addition of beans makes a heartier soup. Makes 6 to 8 servings.

2 lbs. large, ripe Maryland tomatoes
1 large cucumber
1 small onion, finely chopped
1 medium onion
1 green or red pepper
4 cloves garlic, finely chopped
1/4 cup good olive oil
2 Tbsp. red wine vinegar
Salt and pepper to taste
1 cup V-8 juice
1/2 cup fresh basil or 1 tsp. dried basil
Croutons for garnish (optional)
1 can black beans or cannelloni beans (optional)

Finely chop all vegetables and liquify in blender. Add chopped garlic, oil and vinegar, salt, pepper, and basil. Blend into rest of ingredients and add tomato juice. Chill for 4 hours or overnight and serve in bowls with garnish of basil leaves and/or croutons.

Note: If adding optional beans, drain well and mix into soup before refrigerating.

By Mary Lou Baker, Rotary family member

Bread-Tomato Casserole (Brot-Tomaten Auflaue)

Serves 4   Ausgezeichnet!

8-oz. loaf French bread
1 cup white wine
2/3 cup whipping cream
3 tomatoes, sliced
8 oz. Mozzarella cheese, sliced
1 4-oz. can black olives, chopped
1 8-oz. can tomato sauce
3 eggs
1 tsp. Italian seasoning
1/2 tsp. salt and pepper
Parmesan cheese

Cut bread into 1-inch slices and place on cookie sheet. Sprinkle wine and whipping cream over bread and salt lightly. Place all bread except 6 slices into a 2-1/2 qt. casserole. Top with olives and slices of tomatoes and cheese. Lay remaining 6 slices on top. Beat eggs with tomato sauce, Italian seasoning, salt, and pepper and pour over casserole. Sprinkle with Parmesan cheese. Bake in a preheated oven at 320°.

By Ruth Schroeder, Rotary supporter from Ohio

Cranberry-Apple Crisp

3 cups apples (you can also add a cup or two of any frozen fruits)
2-3 cups whole cranberries (buy in fall and keep in freezer)
1-1/3 cup sugar
Mix fruits and sugar and press into greased casserole
Note: A tsp. or two of tapioca keeps it less runny

Topping:
1 stick melted butter   1/2 cup brown sugar
1 cup Quick oats (not instant)   1/2 cup flour
Sliced pecans (optional)

Mix topping ingredients and sprinkle on top of mixture. Bake 1 hour at 350°. Delicious served hot, topped with frozen gelato or ice-cream

By Dean Ebaugh, Rotary supporter

OTHER FAVORITE RECIPES

Rotary members have favorite dishes that range from barbecue sauce reminiscent of the Naptown barBAYq to hearty family recipes. These recipes have been submitted by Parole Rotary Club members and their families, members of other Rotary clubs, and Rotary supporters.

Black Max Barbeque Sauce
This is a variation of a Black Jack sauce given to me by my late brother-in-law, Max Hill. I named it in his honor. It is not nearly as sweet as most commercial sauces. It can be used as a barbeque or grilling sauce and as a condiment for cooked food.

1 cup strong black coffee	1 cup Worcestershire sauce
1 cup catsup	1/2 cup apple cider vinegar
1/2 cup brown sugar	3 Tbsp. chili powder
2 tsp. salt	1 tsp. ground mustard
2 cups chopped onion	6 cloves garlic, minced

Combine all ingredients in a sauce pan, bring to boil, and then simmer for 25 minutes or more. Let cool, then puree in a blender until smooth. (Caution: Hot liquid expands explosively in a blender; let sauce cool prior to blending.)

By Henry Riser, Past and Current President, Parole Rotary Club, and barBAYq Chair

Grilled Pork Sausage with Warm Potato Salad

Cook sausage links on the grill over indirect heat, with the lid closed. Flip after 15 minutes and continue cooking until interior temperature reaches 160°. Move them directly over the fire to crisp for 1-3 minutes until well browned. Turn and brown all sides.

As a side dish, prepare a warm potato salad. Boil 1 ½ pounds of small red potatoes for 10-15 minutes until tender. Mix a dressing using the following ingredients:

1-1/2 Tbsp. Dijon mustard
1 tsp. white wine vinegar
2 Tbsp. finely chopped fresh parsley
3 Tbsp. olive oil
1 tsp. garlic powder

Whisk dressing ingredients in a small bowl. When potatoes are boiled, cut in half and place in a large bowl. Pour dressing over potatoes and toss. Serve as the side dish to the grilled sausages.

By Bob Whitcomb, Rotarian, sailor, and waterways environmentalist

Southern Spoon Bread

Makes 6 to 8 servings

1 cup corn meal
4 Tbsp. butter or margarine
4 cups milk
4 eggs, well beaten
1-1/2 tsp. salt

Preheat oven to 400°. Combine cornmeal, butter or margarine, and 3 cups milk in sauce pan over medium heat. Bring to a boil, stirring constantly. Blend beaten eggs, salt and remaining milk. Add to corn meal mixture; mix well. Pour into greased 2-quart casserole. Bake 45 minutes. Serve hot with butter.

By Virginia Butler, Rotary supporter from Virginia

Baked Grits

This dish should be served from the pan in which it is baked. Cooking grits in milk instead of water gives them a very creamy texture and flavor.

4-1/2 cups milk
1 cup quick grits (not instant)
1/4 cup (1/2 stick) unsalted butter
1 tsp. salt
2 eggs

Preheat oven to 350°. Generously butter a 1-1/2 or 2-quart casserole and set aside. Bring 4 cups of the milk carefully to a boil; do not scorch. Add 1 cup quick grits in a steady stream, stirring all the while. Cook 4 minutes, continuing to stir. Remove from heat and add the butter, salt, and remaining 1/2 cup milk. Mix well. Beat the eggs well and add to the mixture. Mix and pour into the prepared casserole. Bake for 1 hour. While waiting to bake, practice your southern accent!

By Susan Cannon, Rotary supporter from North Carolina

Mexican Spaghetti

Easy, quick, inexpensive, and delicious meal to serve a large crowd in Parole or elsewhere

1 lb. ground beef
1 lb. pork sausage
1 cup chopped onions
1/2 cup chopped peppers (all colors); add Jalapeno pepper if you like it spicy
1 tsp. each salt and pepper
2 tsp. cayenne pepper
2 cups canned tomatoes
1 16-oz. can tomato sauce
1 8-oz. package spaghetti, cooked
1 cup grated cheddar cheese

Brown first four ingredients in heavy skillet, stirring until crumbly, and then drain. Add remaining ingredients except cheese with 1/2 cup water; mix well. Simmer for 10 minutes. Pour into 2-quart buttered casserole. Bake for 20 minutes at 400°. Top with grated cheese. Bake for 10 minutes longer. Enjoy!

By Bertha Garcia, Rotary supporter

Taco Cheese Ball

1 block cream cheese, softened
1 cup shredded pepper jack cheese
1 cup shredded cheddar cheese
1 can any flavor of your choice Rotel tomatoes, drained
1 tsp. taco seasoning
12 tortilla chips, finely crushed
Crackers or cut-up raw vegetables for serving

Beat the cream cheese with other cheeses until well combined. Stir in the tomatoes and taco seasoning. Form into a ball and refrigerate for 1 hour. Roll in the tortilla chips. Serve with veggies and crackers.

By Tony Gonzalez, Rotary supporter

Sauerkraut and Pork (Alsatian)

Das ist Gut!

2 whole onions, skins removed
8 whole cloves
2 carrots, pared
2 lb. sliced bacon, cut in fourths
2-lb. smoked boneless pork butt
10 whole black peppers
4 1-lb. cans sauerkraut (2 qt.), drained
1 Tbsp. butter or margarine
2 14-oz. cans clear chicken broth (3-1/2 cups)
1 cup white wine
1/4 cup lemon juice

Stud each onion with 4 cloves. Put onions, carrots, bacon, and smoked pork butt in large kettle. Add peppers, tied in cheesecloth bag. Cover with sauerkraut; add butter. Combine broth, wine, and lemon juice. Pour over mixture in kettle; bring to boiling point. Reduce heat; simmer, covered, 1-1/2 to 2 hours or until pork butt is fork tender.
Discard onions and cheesecloth bag. Variation: Slice onions thin and cook with sauerkraut, omitting the cloves.

To serve: Cut each piece of bacon into 4 slices and pork butt into 8 slices. Arrange on large platter, with sauerkraut. Slice carrots crosswise and use as garnish.

By Emma Miller, Rotary family member and grandmother of editor Joyce Edelson

Pumpkin-Pecan Spice Bread

Makes one 1-pound loaf, basic bread setting of bread maker

1-3/4 cup bread flour
1/2 cup whole wheat flour
1 Tbsp. unsalted butter or margarine, room temperature
1/2 tsp. salt
1/2 tsp. pumpkin pie spice
1 large egg
1/3 cup milk
1/8 cup orange juice
1/4 cup canned pumpkin
1/4 cup sugar
1/3 cup pecan pieces
1-1/2 to 2 tsp. active dry yeast

Process the ingredients according to manufacturer's instructions for basic bread setting. Remove the bread from the bread pan to a rack to cool. Wrap in aluminum foil or a paper bag to store.

By Jane Frantzich, Rotary family member and retired school administrator

About the Researcher/Editor/Author – Joyce Edelson

Joyce Edelson
Image courtesy of Les Howard Studios

Joyce grew up on a farm in the Midwest, the 6th of 10 children; moved to the Washington, DC area immediately after graduation from high school; had a career in the federal government and is a veteran of Capitol Hill; retired and fulfilled her life-long dream of attending college; earned a B.A. in Psychology from Marymount University and an M.S. in Counseling from Johns Hopkins University.

Past president of Anne Arundel County affiliate of NAMI (National Alliance on Mental Illness); co-facilitates support groups and co-teaches classes for families who have a loved one suffering from mental illness (www.NAMI.org).

Past president of Parole Rotary Club (www.Parole-Rotary.org); served for 12 years as retail chair of Parole Rotary Club's signature project, Books for International Goodwill (B.I.G.) and is a member of its Board of Trustees (www.BIG-books.org)

Joyce volunteered to research history of the Parole Area, interview residents of the area, collect, and write many stories for this book: *Memories and History of Parole Area – Annapolis and Anne Arundel County, Maryland*

Author of *The Rock Creek Shaman*, a spiritual and historical novel, available from her website: (www.JoyceEdelson.com).

Joyce has a son, a son-in-law and 3 grandchildren; resides in Riva, Maryland with her partner Don Gantzer, a retired systems engineer now teaching systems engineering, and two rescue dogs - Summer (a Jack Russell Terrier) and Jackie (a German Pinscher).